P9-DUK-457

About Pfeiffer

Pfeiffer serves the professional development and hands-on resource needs of training and human resource practitioners and gives them products to do their jobs better. We deliver proven ideas and solutions from experts in HR development and HR management, and we offer effective and customizable tools to improve workplace performance. From novice to seasoned professional, Pfeiffer is the source you can trust to make yourself and your organization more successful.

Essential Knowledge Pfeiffer produces insightful, practical, and comprehensive materials on topics that matter the most to training and HR professionals. Our Essential Knowledge resources translate the expertise of seasoned professionals into practical, how-to guidance on critical workplace issues and problems. These resources are supported by case studies, worksheets, and job aids and are frequently supplemented with CD-ROMs, Web sites, and other means of making the content easier to read, understand, and use.

Essential Tools Pfeiffer's Essential Tools resources save time and expense by offering proven, ready-to-use materials—including exercises, activities, games, instruments, and assessments—for use during a training or team-learning event. These resources are frequently offered in loose-leaf or CD-ROM format to facilitate copying and customization of the material.

Pfeiffer also recognizes the remarkable power of new technologies in expanding the reach and effectiveness of training. While e-hype has often created whizbang solutions in search of a problem, we are dedicated to bringing convenience and enhancements to proven training solutions. All our e-tools comply with rigorous functionality standards. The most appropriate technology wrapped around essential content yields the perfect solution for today's on-the-go trainers and human resource professionals.

Essential resources for training and HR professionals

Getting the Most from Online Learning

Getting the Most from Online Learning

George M. Piskurich
Editor

Published by Pfeiffer
An Imprint of Wiley
989 Market Street, San Francisco, CA94103-1741 · www.pfeiffer.com

For additional copies/bulk purchases of this book in the U.S. please contact 800-274-4434.

Pfeiffer books and products are available through most bookstores. To contact Pfeiffer directly call our Customer Care Department within the U.S. at 800-274-4434, outside the U.S. at 317-572-3985 or fax 317-572-4002 or www.pfeiffer.com.

Pfeiffer also publishes its books in a variety of electronic formats. Some content that appears in print may not be available in electronic books.

Library of Congress Cataloging-in-Publication Data

Getting the most from online learning / [edited by] George Piskurich.—
1st ed.
p. cm.
Includes bibliographical references and index.
ISBN 0-7879-6504-9 (alk. paper)
1. Education—Computer network resources. 2. Business—Computer network resources. 3. Internet in education. I. Piskurich, George M.
LB1044.87.G48 2002
371.33'4678—dc21

2003011728

Acquiring Editor: Lisa Shannon
Director of Development: Kathleen Dolan Davies
Developmental Editor: Susan Rachmeler
Editor: Rebecca Taff
Senior Production Editor: Justin Frahm
Manufacturing Supervisor: Bill Matherly
Cover Design: Chris Wallace

Printed in the United States of America

Printing 10 9 8 7 6 5 4 3 2 1

Contents

Introduction

I'D LIKE TO START BY SAYING that this is one of a number of good books on the topic of e-learning that have been published lately; but in all honesty, there haven't been that many. Basically, the discipline is too new and changing too rapidly for there to be a large body of writings concerning it. Therefore, what you are now reading may not only be the best book on this particular aspect of e-learning, but possibly the only one that really looks at e-learning from the learner's perspective.

Getting the Most from Online Learning originated in another book I had the privilege to edit, *Preparing Learners for E-Learning*. The last chapter in that book was a collection of comments that we received from e-learners detailing their experiences with e-learning. To say that they were enlightening would be an understatement. Many of the things that we knew could be problems with e-learning, but that we had thought were transparent to the learners, really were not. Other problems that we had never even considered kept appearing again and again in those comments.

We realized that if the learners had this many problems, complaints, and criticisms concerning the process, a book that would help them to personally prepare for e-learning was just as critical as the one we'd just finished that detailed how organizations and instructors could prepare their employees for e-learning. And so we have produced the book you now hold, *Getting the Most from Online Learning*. It is a companion volume to *Preparing Learners for E-Learning*, but stands on its own as well for any current or would be e-learner.

If you've come this far and now find yourself asking, "But why would I be interested in learning to be an e-learner?" then you should probably put this book down and find another. But I caution you that, if you do, you will be turning your back on what will no doubt be the future of a majority of your learning—and possibly your future as well. Your school or organization may not have an e-learning process today, but they will tomorrow, and it will be your responsibility to use it effectively. That's what e-learning is about—the learner taking on more responsibility for the learning.

And if you don't care about work or school, I refer you to the Internet. There is already more information on the Web concerning you and your life than you could ever hope to master, and it grows every day. E-Learning is how you use the Web to obtain that information and put it to use for you and your family. And this book will help you prepare to learn from the Web.

PURPOSE AND AUDIENCE

The purpose of this book is to help learners to help themselves become better e-learners by providing them with information on how to prepare for, participate in, and apply e-learning in all its variations. It serves as a companion volume to *Preparing Learners for E-Learning*, which considers the topic from the view of designers, instructors, and administrators. Naturally, the audience for the book is the e-learner, brand-new to e-learning or somewhat experienced, but either way looking for ways to make his or her learning more effective.

The secondary audience is those of us who create e-learning, either as designers developing programs or as administrators originating and managing e-learning for an organization. No matter which of these roles you fill, it is critical for you to be aware of what an e-learner must know and do to succeed in the world of e-learning.

SCOPE AND TREATMENT

The information presented here is not theory. It is practical knowledge won the hard way, through experience. All of the authors have both experienced e-learning personally and worked with their learners as they mastered the process for themselves as part of the e-learning initiatives that they (our authors) created.

In their chapters the authors present their unique viewpoints on what they observed their learners doing to become effective e-learners, and they explain how you can use what they learned to make yourself a better e-learner. The richness of their experiences as e-learning experts is evident in every part of the book.

Each chapter is different, not only because it focuses in on a different aspect of being an e-learner, but because each author will speak to you from his or her own experience in working with e-learners. Whether you need to learn (1) the best approach for preparing for a synchronous class, (2) how to handle online learning relationships, or (3) techniques for managing distractions while you are taking your e-learning classes, you'll find it here, covered the way you need it, from the perspective of the e-learner.

HOW TO READ THIS BOOK

As a reader you will probably want to pick and choose chapters to read, depending on your personal needs. For example, you may be beginning an asynchronous course next week and choose to look through Chapter 6, or you may have been asked to be part of an online group learning project, and thus review Chapter 11.

If you are interested in everything about how to use e-learning effectively, you might read the book from cover to cover. But as with most things in our busy lives, it is usually best to start with the things you need to know now and work toward those you are just curious about. Since each of our chapters can stand on its own, that shouldn't be a problem. Read the content synopsis that follows and choose your own beginning.

CONTENT SUMMARY

This book contains a glossary of terms to help you work your way through the many-faceted process that we term *e-learning*. The definitions have been provided by our author experts and can be referred to whenever a term is new to you or whenever you are interested in how we define a concept.

Our first chapter sets the tone for the book by "taking the issue to the people that matter most" as it discusses some of the preparation issues raised by e-learners in their own words. Janet Piskurich relates her learners' comments on their preparation techniques and what they have done to make themselves successful e-learners. In case you find that these comments also reflect your own thoughts on e-learning, we've noted the chapters of the book that relate to them with each comment.

Chapter 2 introduces (or for some re-introduces) us to what e-learning actually is. Dr. Huey Long takes us back to the origins of e-learning, provides us a general definition so we all know what we are talking about, and discusses some of the advantages of e-learning for everyone, but particularly for the learner.

Paul and Lucy Guglielmino are up next. Their discussion on how to make yourself more self-directed as a part of your e-learning preparation can help you become a more effective and happier e-learner.

In Chapter 4 Bill Knapp gives you the lowdown on how to prepare to attend a synchronous (live) e-learning class. The topics he discusses, such as how to get comfortable with the technology and preparing the proper e-learning environment, will help you to get ready to get the most out of being online in a live, instructor-led, e-learning program.

Bill also wrote Chapter 5. This time he takes you on to the next step of how to actually participate in a live e-learning session. He provides you with ideas on concepts such as how to make the best use of common software capabilities, how to interact effectively with other e-classroom colleagues, and how to get ready for your next synchronous session.

The other half of e-learning is asynchronous programming, that is, learning in which there is no instructor, but only you and the computer. In Chapter 6 Harvey Singh considers the techniques that will make you a better asynchronous e-learner. He explains how the asynchronous environment is different for a learner and provides you with information on the seven habits of highly effective asynchronous learners.

Chapter 7 looks at how the e-learner should prepare for and participate in two of the most common aspects of e-learning: discussion boards and chat rooms.

A key aspect of e-learning is the online readings that you find with almost every program—and certainly wherever you go on the Web. In Chapter 8 Ryan Watkins shows you how to make the most of these readings and provides you with information on the technology that makes them work and with techniques for increasing your effectiveness in using them.

Chapter 9 deals with a relatively new aspect of e-learning: peer evaluation. Russ Brock gives us an incisive explanation on what peer evaluations are all about, how they are used and abused, and a host of techniques for how to be a better peer evaluator and evaluatee.

In Chapter 10 Doug Liberati discusses another key issue for e-learning, or e-anything for that matter: how to form and nurture good online relationships. He provides an extensive list of tips on how to interact online, the use of emoticons, how to work in an online team, and some do's and don'ts for online chat. He also discusses the negative side of the process and tells you what you can do when your online e-learning relationships are on the rocks.

In Chapter 11, Carole Richardson takes the lead from Doug and provides more detail on how to work as a member of an online learning team or group. She talks about the various group tools, such as discussion boards, chat rooms, and e-mail, then gives you a model to use for the initiation and development of any online group. She also provides you with a great personal checklist for evaluating your own online group skills.

One of the major complaints of e-learners is that they simply have no place to do their learning where they are not being constantly interrupted. You may never be able to completely solve this problem, but in Chapter 12 Wayne Turmel gives you some techniques on how to whittle it down to size. He first discusses the various categories of distractions and what causes them. Then he looks at what you, the e-learner, can do to deal with them, and he finishes up with what you can ask your organization to do as well.

So there you have it, just what a learner needs to know to become a successful e-learner. If you're only considering becoming an e-learner, or you have been informed that you *will* be one as your organization is requiring it, you may want to read this book from front to back. On the other hand, if you are already engaged in e-learning and just want to increase your effectiveness, you may choose to read only those chapters that pertain to your current e-learning activities. But either way, we hope that what we've provided for you in this book will help you get the most from your e-learning experiences.

About the Editor

George M. Piskurich is an organizational learning and performance consultant, specializing in e-learning interventions, performance analysis, and telecommuting. His workshops on self-directed learning, structured mentoring, and preparing learners for e-learning have been rated "outstanding" by participants from many organizations.

With more than twenty-five years of experience in learning technology, he has been a classroom instructor, training manager, instructional designer, and e-learning consultant for multinational clients and smaller organizations. He has created classroom seminars, OJT mentoring systems, and e-learning interventions.

He has been a presenter and workshop leader at more than thirty conferences and symposia, and is an active member of both ISPI and ASTD.

He has written books on instructional technology, self-directed learning, instructional design and telecommuting, authored journal articles and book chapters on various topics, and is currently editing two books on e-learning. In 1986 he was ASTD's "Instructional Technologist of the Year," and won the "Best Use of Instructional Technology in Business" award in 1992.

Getting the Most from Online Learning

Chapter 1

Voices from the Edge of E-Learning

Janet F. Piskurich

AN EDGE IS A LINEAR SURFACE where something begins (or ends). For e-learning, it is that fragile interface between the e-learning and the e-learner. What is it that e-learners say about their experience with walking this line? What can those who have been at the edge tell us about what they did to succeed?

In the last chapter of this book's companion volume, *Preparing Learners for E-Learning*, we recorded some comments from e-learners that we had gathered while working on the project. We thought that a collection of structured responses from e-learners concerning the ways they prepare for e-learning would make an appropriate chapter for this book. The learners in our survey experienced a learning environment in which e-learning was encouraged as a means of preparing them to be lifelong learners in the rapidly changing field of medicine. We created a questionnaire but, knowing how busy these e-learners were, there were only two questions:

- Do you feel that you successfully prepared yourself to use the electronic resources that are available to you? If so, how?
- Are there things that you feel you or others could have done to prepare you more effectively for e-learning?

We think you'll find that what these e-learners said can be of great help to you; and to assist you even further we've noted the chapters of the book that relate to them with each comment.

***"It's hard at first, but stay with it."* (Chapters 3, 12, and 13)**

The learners noted that it isn't easy to become an e-learner. The classroom does not prepare you for being responsible for your own learning. You need to expect to have a difficult time, to meet with failure, and to experience times when you "just don't feel like doing it," but you need to work through those times. Once you know what to expect of the programs and of yourself, it becomes easier.

"The first part of e-learning is learning to use the software."

"Software is the hardest part."

"Experience with the software will make you more comfortable with it."

***"Once you master the software, learning the content material comes easy."* (Chapters 4 and 6)**

You need to sit down and learn the software before you engage in a learning program. This will make you much more comfortable when you do your learning. There are many different types of software programs in e-learning, but they all follow the same basic approach, so when you learn one you have a leg up on them all. The wrong time to learn about software capabilities is after you've already spent a lot of time using it and now find out that you could have or need to do other things to make your learning effective. A lot of programs are written with bad navigation functions, which makes them much harder to use. Forget about what you've seen before and would like to be able to do with this software and settle down to do what you can. Otherwise you just get frustrated and quit. Synchronous software is much harder to use and requires more time. If they give you a chance to practice, take it, particularly if there is someone around during the practice who can answer your questions. Don't be afraid to ask questions, particularly about what you'd like the software to do. Sometimes it's there but hidden, and if you find out about it you can save a lot of time and effort.

"Having experience with computers, any computers for any reason, is a major advantage."

You don't need to be a software whiz, or even a keyboard whiz, to use e-learning effectively, but it helps a lot if you understand a little about computers. Being used to the quirks of computers, the possible bugs, and the times when they just lock up and refuse to let you go on can save you a lot of aggravation and the desire to quit the e-learning program. Knowing how to use a mouse helps, and if the program isn't good, knowing how to get around its problems is helpful too. Simply being used to sitting at a keyboard and watching a monitor is a big help, particularly for those long, boring programs.

"Being comfortable with learning on your own makes it easier to succeed at e-learning."

"If you are used to having a teacher tell you everything, you need to break that mold first."

"Use the Web to help you learn to learn on your own!" (Chapters 3 and 6)

The hardest thing in e-learning is to realize that there is no instructor there for most of the time. If you like to learn on your own, you're far ahead; but if you like an instructor to tell you what's important, you need to get used to the idea of the program being your guide. Get used to looking over the program first and reading that stuff they put in the introduction that you usually ignore. That helps you teach yourself. If you have the chance to do something where it's both e-learning and an instructor, do it. Then ask the instructor what you should have learned. Simply surfing the Web can help you prepare for e-learning. Make a goal and use the Web to achieve it for practice.

"Initially, finding the right resources is the hard part. Once you start e-learning you develop a curiosity to find new resources." (Chapters 7, 8, 10, and 11)

In some situations you need to find your own learning resources or go to places where the program points you, but find your own answers. These are the hardest if you're not used to it, but it becomes easier once you do it. You will find that the more you do it the more you like it. Sometimes you end up going way beyond what they want you to do, but that's all right too, as long as you don't forget that you still need to take the test at the end. So budget your time wisely.

"Over time you'll not only become good at it but you won't want to do without e-learning." (Chapters 2 and 13)

The neat part about e-learning is that you become addicted to it. It is hard to get started, and you feel real uncomfortable at first as it seems you're out there all alone, but once you know you can learn on your own you begin to like it. Then you realize that you don't want to go back to the other way, don't want to sit in a class at a specific time and learn only what you are told. It's freedom!

"I learned by trial and error and word of mouth, which isn't the best way. Look for a coach or mentor who can help you become a more efficient e-learner." (Chapters 7, 9, 10, and 11)

Most e-learners learn by doing it, which isn't bad, but it isn't good either. There is a lot you can learn from those who have already done it if you can talk to them, so make an effort. Find a buddy who has already done it and ask for advice. Find someone you can call when you have a question or problem. Don't just jump into it; read the directions first. It will save you time and aggravation in the end.

"I found that e-learning provides me with easier, faster, and more up-to-date content than classrooms." (Chapters 2, 5, and 7)

The neat thing about e-learning is that once you get used to using it the right way, you can always find the most up-to-date stuff. Sometimes this is material that even your instructors don't know, and you can be impressive as heck with it. It also gets to be easier to just find the answers on your own. Once you are sure of your e-learning abilities, you don't need to wait for someone else to provide the answers.

And the single comment most often made by our e-learners:

"The only way to get good at it is to practice using it." (Chapters 2, 3, 5, 6, and 11)

This is the key to e-learning. To learn to do it you've got to do it. Don't get frustrated and give up. Don't say you'd rather have someone tell you what you need to know. Don't kick your computer when it locks up and decide the whole idea is stupid. Use it, use it again, and use it some more. It is hard at first, but it gets easier, and then it gets great. Even if you have mentors, good instructions, and computer skills, you still need to practice using a system to use it well, because it's as individual as you are, and you'll use it differently than everyone else. So keep at it until you're good.

Like the highwire artist who walks across a tiny strand of metal far above the crowd, e-learners need practice on the edge. Some require a harness at first while others prefer to plunge headlong into the net when they fall off, but they all agree that you need to keep going back and that the practice it takes to become a successful e-learner is well worth the effort!

About the Author

Janet F. Piskurich, Ph.D., is a research scientist and educator on the faculty at Mercer University School of Medicine in Macon, Georgia. Although heavily involved in research related to the control of immune responses, she also tutors first-year and second-year medical students in several phases of the biological science curriculum and is involved in teaching various workshops for both children and adults. Her interest in self-direction in learners is reflected by the problem-based learning methodology she employs in her teaching.

Along with numerous scientific publications, she has authored articles and book chapters on self-directed learning and individualized career development. She holds a B.S. degree from the University of Pittsburgh and a doctorate in experimental pathology and immunology from Case Western Reserve University, Cleveland, Ohio. She can be reached at (478) 301–4035 or via e-mail at Piskurich_J@Mercer.edu.

Chapter 2

E-Learning

An Introduction

Huey B. Long

EVEN A CURSORY REVIEW of the e-learning field will reveal how plentiful the options are. With so many programs available, how can you decide what is best for you? While cost, time, and reputation are important, you also need to consider your personal learning style. If you are a prospective or beginning e-learner, you should consider three important questions: (1) Is e-learning for you? (2) What do you know about e-learning? and (3) What should you know? To determine whether e-learning is for you, you need the answers to the two questions: What do you know? and What should you know about e-learning? This chapter is designed to help you answer those questions.

There is much to be known concerning e-learning, but it is not necessary to know all of it to be a successful e-learner. There are seven topical areas with which you should have at least a minimal awareness: (1) a definition of e-learning, (2) e-learning advantages, (3) potential problem areas, (4) the importance of e-learning in contemporary times, (5) the scope and status of e-learning as an educational and training method, (6) e-learning modes, and (7) assessment results.

We begin with a definition followed by a discussion of e-learning advantages and potential problem areas. Then recent trends that illustrate the importance of e-learning are noted, after which you will be introduced to a brief discussion of the scope and status of e-learning. Next you will learn about e-learning modes and some assessment results and opinions. Finally, a summary and concluding comments close the chapter. In an effort to further illustrate the usefulness of e-learning, much of the chapter content is based on material readily available electronically.

A DEFINITION OF e-LEARNING

It would be difficult for you to have a productive understanding of e-learning without a workable definition, but we are faced with the danger of loading the manuscript down with definitions or being too parsimonious with the task. We hope that the following explanation is adequate for your use. Stated very simply, *e-learning is any learning that is based on the use of electronic media*. Yet it seemed that a little more was required; therefore, we selected the following definition instead:

> e-Learning is defined as: *any form of learning that utilizes a network for delivery, interaction, or facilitation* (in a few years you might not even use the computer). The network could be the Internet, a school or college LAN or even a complete WAN. The learning could take place individually (guided or instructed by a computer) or as part of a class. Online classes meet either synchronously (at the same time) or asynchronously (at different times), or some combination of the two. (e-learner.com, 2000, para 2)

The definition is broad, but a broadly inclusive definition is needed to establish the boundaries of the topic. It simply means that the term *e-learning* currently refers to learning that occurs as a result of information obtained via an electronic means and that the process may include diverse formats and procedures. While e-learning certainly can include autodidactic Web-based inquiry, this chapter focuses mostly on online courses. More is said about this later, especially in the section concerning e-learning modes. The following comments on the scope and status of e-learning illustrate the opportunities available to you as an e-learner.

ADVANTAGES OF E-LEARNING

Many advantages to e-learning may accrue to individual learners and to institutions. Since institutions such as corporations, schools, and colleges seem to be the stimulators of e-learning interests, we'll first look at the benefits to them. Then we'll identify and discuss the learner advantages.

Institutional Advantages

Corporations and educational institutions identify a variety of justifications for e-learning. Four of the reasons for the acceptance, development, and expansion of e-learning are discussed.

1. *International business:* The trend toward global business set the stage for the delivery of training via electronic means.
2. *Speed of development and delivery*: Many corporations have found that paper- and platform- (classroom) based training was obsolete by the time the courseware was developed and distributed. Electronic-based material meets the just-in-time learning needs of the corporation better than much of the formerly provided classroom instruction.
3. *Flexibility:* E-Learning can be used by managers and other employees according to their own schedules and at dispersed locations.
4. *Cost savings:* The prospect of savings has attracted great attention. IBM is reported to have estimated savings of $175 million in 1999, computed at $490 per student day in avoiding such expenses as travel, course fees, and other inefficiencies of classroom instruction. Cisco Systems reportedly saves at least $240 million annually, allocated at $12,000 per year for each employee who previously would have attended four classes a year. One training-research organization estimates that companies experience a 40 to 60 percent cost saving when moving from classroom- to technology-based training

(Terry, 2000). The DOW Chemical Corporation devised a corporate-wide training system known as Learn@dow.now in 1999. The system cost $1.3 million initially and requires $600,000 in annual maintenance cost. Over forty thousand employees took and passed a six-hour course between October 2000 and February 2001 at a saving of nearly $2.7 million (Overby, 2002).

It should not be surprising that some of the institutional advantages are reflected in the following learner advantages discussed.

Personal Learner Advantages

Individual, as well as institutional, advantages also are attributed to e-learning. Seven advantages often mentioned are as follows:

1. Reduced travel time and costs for learners
2. Self-paced learning whereby learners can control their schedules
3. Convenience of any time and any place
4. Opportunity for repeated practice
5. Ease of review
6. Self-responsibility, and
7. Freedom

Let's examine these advantages in some detail in the order in which they are listed. First, for more than fifty years adults have cited two major obstacles to continuing to learn: lack of time and lack of money (or the cost is too great). E-Learning addresses both of these obstacles. It may be less difficult to go to your computer desk at home or work than to travel across town or even to another building in your work complex. As a result, you may save time and the expenses associated with travel. (Of course, there are some potential problems associated with the same phenomena. For example, computer access and family or other social distractions may complicate study at home.)

The second and third advantages occur mostly with asynchronous modes. In such modes you are not obligated to "meet" with an instructor or trainer at a specific time. If you travel and work at different locations, you may not be able to engage in traditional place-based educational or training activities. A potential challenge, however, is presented by the freedom found in e-learning. More is said about this later.

The fourth and fifth advantages are dependent on specific formats and content. For example, the popular computer software training packages based on CDs provide unlimited opportunity to practice different applications. Typing programs provide opportunities to practice keystrokes. Virtual reality-based programs as used in health care and in the military also provide safe practice opportunities that would not be readily available in other modes. Thus, the availability of similar practice and review opportunities will vary with the kind of e-learning you choose.

It is readily apparent that e-learning encourages and requires self-responsibility. If you are the type of person who needs the structure of a definite meeting time and place, as is common to traditional learning, you may need to change your lifestyle and preferences to accommodate the new freedom associated with e-learning. It is common knowledge that learner dropout rates are higher in e-learning college courses than in traditional courses, showing that not everyone has the self-responsibility required.

The seventh learner advantage is potentially the most powerful. If you are a highly motivated learner who is comfortable with the asynchronous mode, you can use e-learning in an autodidactic manner that frees you from the expectations, requirements, and routines of other more powerful people. You choose the topic, you determine the time, you set the criteria for success, and so forth.

While this extreme freedom is likely to be practiced by only a few learners, the option is always available to anyone with the appropriate technology and the requisite personal characteristics.

POTENTIAL PROBLEM AREAS

Given the advantages associated with e-learning, you may have decided that e-learning is for you. There are, however, also some hazards in e-learning of which you should be aware. We've hinted at some of these in the discussion, but let's make them more explicit here. Five major assumptions that may affect your success in e-learning are as follows:

1. The assumption that e-learning requires much less time than traditional educational methods
2. The assumption that because of flexible time and schedules you need not plan your e-learning activities in advance
3. The assumption that you have the personal characteristics and motivation to study and practice in a highly independent mode
4. The assumption that you have the necessary prerequisite skills and knowledge, and
5. The assumption that any and all e-learning programs are legitimate and reputable

The first two assumptions are incorrect if you are engaged in a reputable e-learning program. Legitimate e-learning programs, especially those related to some form of certification or diploma, require comparable time for study and practice as is required in traditional face-to-face instruction. E-Learners may actually find it more challenging to study and practice when there is no set meeting time. With respect to the next two assumptions, if you do not have the requisite personality and knowledge level for e-learning, you are likely to experience problems. E-Learning might not be a good choice for a learner who does best when interacting with an instructor and others in a more formal classroom setting.

Before you decide to enroll in an e-learning program, if you have an option, we recommend a personal analysis of your qualifications. Strong evidence indicates that successful e-learning requires a high commitment and drive as well as acceptance of responsibility to work alone. In addition, e-learning requires learners to make their own arrangements to gain hands-on experience, including accessing equipment and software, and to make the effort to find support when needed. If you don't have these characteristics, e-learning may not be the best choice for you.

The last assumption can cost you quite a bit of money if you fail to do your homework before enrolling in an e-learning program. Because of increasing emphasis on certificates, diplomas, and degrees in the workplace, a number of bogus online schools have emerged. Some of these do little more than take your money and sell degrees. Go to http://distancelearn.about.com to see a Web article entitled "Sixteen Red Flags for Recognizing a Bogus Online School." In case the information has been removed from the Web site, the first five items in that article are as follows:

1. Is the name of the school similar to a well-known reputable university?
2. Is the Web site comprehensive or is the site merely an online brochure?
3. Does the Web site display a photograph of a sample diploma?
4. Is the address for the school a post office box or suite number?
5. Can degrees be earned in less time than at a traditional university?

In addition to these red flags, watch out for suggestions that you do not have to meet any admission requirements, complete no tests, and do no work. Other warning signs include offers to give credit for experience and to sell academic honors. Some bogus online schools learned their sales skills before e-learning became popular, so be careful. Also note that institutions that offer other kinds of education and training courses and who have been in business for several years may be better choices than new, relatively unknown institutions. Finally, be cautious when dealing with unsolicited spam touting online learning.

IMPORTANCE OF E-LEARNING IN CONTEMPORARY TIMES

Understanding some of the factors that have contributed to the growing popularity of e-learning might be helpful to you in your e-learning efforts. Even though your motivation to learn may be narrowly personal, it is probably similar to that of thousands of other people. The reasons for the rush into the provision of online courses, online degrees, training programs, and so forth may be found in recent social and economic developments. The transition of education and training to commodities and learners to consumers (Long, 1987) provides one fundamental explanation. The salience of continuing education and training and current emphasis on human capital, information, and technology have created a demand for education and training, and all kinds of providers have emerged to address the demand.

Various aspects of e-learning, e-education, Web-based education, computer-based instruction, distance education, distance learning, electronic learning, and sundry other references to the new learning media are promoted in an explosion of articles, book chapters, and electronic messages. One Web site identifies 2,400 degree programs, 1,600 schools, and 25,000 online e-learning courses (Offerings, 2002). Because of the attention devoted to e-learning, it is increasingly difficult to navigate the Internet when searching for the best and most recent information. Furthermore, many print items are already out of date when published. The sources, however, indicate corporations and higher education will spend billions of dollars on e-learning in the immediate future (Eduventures releases . . . , 2001). The rapid evolution of the PC (personal computer) and the Internet added new powerful products, processes, and media to the mix. By 2000, American universities were proclaiming the virtues of computer-based delivery. Nearly 75 percent of colleges and universities offered online courses in 1999—up from 48 percent in 1998.

e-Learning has been hailed as the greatest development in learning since the printing press; also, it has been roundly criticized and confusion surrounds many aspects of e-learning because technology, policy, and strategy are not evolving at the same rate. In the year 2002 it is safe to assert that technology is developing faster than other critical e-learning elements. Consequently, the area is characterized by significant disparities in the sophistication of e-learning applications. They range from science-fiction types of simulations in virtual environments to the use of CD-ROM and videotape media that are little more than digital workbooks (Ehrmann, 2001).

SCOPE AND STATUS OF e-LEARNING

Attempting to describe the state of e-learning is similar to eating spaghetti with a knife and Jell-O with chopsticks. The constant changes coming from new technology, hardware, and software, respectively, are changing the landscape almost daily. Since 1999 the number of colleges and universities offering online courses has increased dramatically. More than two million learners were predicted to be enrolled in distance learning programs by 2002 (Cohn, 2000). Nearly 40 percent of venture capital going into the education market went into companies developing e-learning products and services. In 2001 there were five thousand companies offering e-training technology, service, and content. Revenues were projected to reach $2 billion in 2000 and reach $11 billion in 2003 (Cohn, 2002). *Training* magazine predicts the market will be at least $11.5 billion (Desktop distance learning, 2002, para 7). Government contracts often obligate contractors with federal departments to include the Internet and computer-based curricula in their programs of study. At this time, distance education included the computer-based programs. In 1999, U.S. corporations spent $66 billion on training. About 20 percent of that was expended on e-learning and about 80 percent on traditional classroom instruction. Stacy (2000) reported a projected shift to 60 percent e-learning and 40 percent classroom instruction by 2003.

The potential e-learning market is revealed by the trend data for corporate adoption of e-learning. In only one year, the percentage of companies using e-learning for employee training increased by 8 percent, from 16 percent in 2000 to 24 percent in 2001 (*CIO* magazine, 2001). International Data Corporation speculates that the e-learning market, valued at $550 million in 1998, will explode to $7.1 billion in 2002 (www.businessweek.com, 2002). NCR Corporation has developed a virtual campus of 3,600 courses in seventeen languages accessible to employees on the company intranet (Desktop distance learning, 2000, para 4). *Training* magazine is cited as estimating that U.S. organizations budgeted $54 billion for training in 2000, with $19.3 billion going to outside providers of services and products (Desktop distance learning, 2000, para 7).

The Massie Center, a technology and learning think tank, reported that 92 percent of large organizations offered some form of online learning in 1999. The center predicted that many of those companies would be using e-learning throughout their organization by 2002. Some corporations are committing themselves to deliver as much as half of their training online. For example, Motorola mandated that 30 percent of all training be delivered via alternative delivery methods by 2001; that figure was to be increased to 50 percent by 2002. Despite the rate at which e-learning has been embraced by corporations, Terry (2000) indicated that many executives thought the approach was conservative, meaning the market would expand much more in the near future. Some corporate leaders are awaiting more data concerning the advantages and cost/ benefits of e-learning.

E-LEARNING MODES

What e-learning mode appeals to you? Don't be embarrassed if you can't answer the question, but it is important to know. The following paragraphs should help you to understand the various modes available as well as help you state your preference.

E-Learning has been used to refer to various delivery modes, media formats or products, and delivery processes. The broadest categories are *asynchronous* and *synchronous* modes. As indicated by their names, these two modes of e-learning are characterized by the nature of learner-facilitator interaction. In the former, the contribution of the facilitator is temporally static. The information is presented (usually in some recorded format) and the learner can interact with it at any time thereafter. The interaction may be in the form of workbook (print) completion or online recording of responses. A human may review these responses or they may be evaluated by electronic means. Feedback may be provided by a human or via electronically programmed means. In the synchronous mode, the learner and facilitator interact directly. Either may instantaneously provide feedback. "Active online communication" is another way to refer to the synchronous mode. Asynchronous formats may also use online communication, of course, but the online learner activity usually is a response to stored data rather than communication with a human facilitator. Prerecorded and canned programs are typical of the asynchronous mode.

Many, but not all, academic courses and training programs are designed in a manner that does not involve two-way communication between the learner and the developer(s) of the product. In contrast, the use of chat rooms, online dialogue among learners and between learners and the facilitator, are typical of the synchronous mode. Figure 2.1 summarizes various types of e-learning modes, media, and characteristics.

Figure 2.1. Types of E-Learning

Modes	Media	Format	Characteristics
Asynchronous	Computer CD/disks/online	Structured/ unstructured	Individual interaction
	Radio	Structured	Individual interaction
	Television, satellites/videotapes	Structured	Individual interaction
Synchronous	Computer online chat rooms/ shared whiteboards/ application sharing/ television and videoconferencing	Structured	Interpersonal interaction
	Radio, special crystal, dedicated line	Structured	Interpersonal interaction
	Television, satellite or dedicated line, television and videoconferencing	Structured	Interpersonal interaction

The asynchronous media are available for random selection and use, whereas the synchronous media are usually limited to systematic use. For example, you may purchase a computer instructional program and use that product in a random fashion to address problems as they occur; of course, you may use the same product in a systematic manner. In either case, however, you do not interact with another human at the time of practice or application. In addition, you may pursue learning based on the World Wide Web (WWW) in a random manner. Synchronous media usually require the learner to engage in the program in a prescribed manner for enrollment, participation in chat rooms, whiteboards, shared applications, group projects, individual activities, and evaluation activities.

Industry projections indicate the future growth of synchronous media will greatly exceed the asynchronous. Growth in the use of CD-ROM, videotape, and satellite media will account for a decreasing share of the activity by 2004 (Mayor, 2000). A significant debate revolves around who will be the future developers of the media. Will corporations and educational institutions develop the media in-house or outsource it?

ASSESSMENT

E-Learning is not devoid of numerous ethical issues. The profundity of ethical questions increases directly with the degree that providers of e-learning programs and materials have conflicting interests. What safeguards can institutions devise that isolate them from producing, promoting, and benefiting from shoddy products? As we mentioned previously, e-learning opportunities are provided by a very large segment of the education establishment, and even reputable institutions have a motive to offer inadequately designed e-learning courses. Given the institutional and professional conflicts of interests and the rush to be first with the most, how can learners be assured of the appropriateness and effectiveness of e-learning?

Candidly, it is well known that the education establishment has consistently failed to satisfactorily exploit and apply technology to learning. Educators generally have lacked the knowledge and technocrats have been ignorant of learning theory (Willison, 2001). Chickering and Ehrman (1996) note that we have been expecting a computer-enabled revolution in teaching and learning in higher education for forty years. They attribute past failures to inappropriate strategies, not to the technology. Willison thinks e-learning isn't all its cracked up to be. He notes that too many of the e-learning products don't contain much information and that what information they have lacks authority. He suggests that many lessons and products are no more than electronic text material. While this is true, we should not assume that all e-learning courses are simply text-based. Ehrmann (2001) is critical of the failure of IT to meet expectations in higher education. Among other shortcomings, he notes that educators have been overly awed by technology and have forgotten that the speed of technological change is often faster than the time it takes higher education to implement procedures.

While everyone may be convinced of the value of e-learning, Dave Siefert, director of NCR University Virtual Learning, which offers six hundred Web-based courses, reported a recent cost/benefit analysis of all types of technology-oriented training based on a survey of 288 employees. The analysis showed that Web-based training delivered nine times the benefits over the costs in terms of productivity and the quality of the experience (Berry, 1999).

Capitalworks LLC, a human capital management service, issued a contrarian view, however. They said that companies funding formalized e-training programs would have been better off spending their money on less costly informal and self-study methods (Kounadis, 2001). Informal methods were shown to increase employee knowledge and productivity far more than formal educational methods. Their study thus confirms that new employment skills are learned informally through discussions with coworkers and mentoring by managers, supervisors, and others. Only about 25 percent of employee skills in the study were learned from formal training methods such as workshops, seminars, and classes.

Redding and Rotzien (2000) reported a comparison of learners involved in a pre-licenser program offered by two methods. One group of learners was in a traditional classroom-based community college course; the other was enrolled in an online course offered by the community college. E-Learners performed better and were reported to have better cognitive understanding of the subject. In contrast, a Gartner Group study reported that 150 recent e-learners rated the quality of instructor-led training 0.5 to 1.5 points higher on a scale of 1 to 10 than they did online instruction. E-Learning was rated higher in cost and time to learn effectively (Terry, 2000).

CONCLUSION

Recent advances in technology present astounding opportunities for education and training, but the opportunities bring profound challenges. Rapidly expanding information requires a highly informed workforce and citizenry who need more than traditional approaches to training and education. Yet the need cannot be met by merely placing a veneer of technology over an inadequate traditional approach. Technology is available to revolutionize training, education, teaching, and learning. It will not be a simple matter of transporting text from lecture notes and print media to simulations and virtual environments supported by robotics and other hardware. Neither will it be inexpensive. But the increasing use of servers to store and communicate advances and modification can be incorporated into systems at reduced costs.

At this time, it seems prudent to conclude that e-learning is e-learning as a rose is a rose. There are some exceptionally good examples available. There are also some awful products. Some are difficult to navigate, and others are merely typescripts presented in a digital manner. Asynchronous formats also present problems for learners who have already mastered much of the "canned" program material. While it appears that there are more favorable comments than negative ones, major work is needed before e-learning achieves its potential. Yet it seems that the number of good simulations and the sense-enriched programs are increasing, along with the development of virtual environment based products.

References

Berry, J. (1999). *Web learning starts to pay off. Companies say web training is cheaper and more measurable*. [Retrieved October, 3, 2001, from www.techweb .com.html.]

Chickering, A., & Ehrman, S. C. (1996, October). Implementing the seven principles: Technology as lever. *AAHE Bulletin*, pp. 3–6.

Cohn, B. (2000, September 1). *The ABC's of e-learning*. [Retrieved March 11, 2002, from www. Theindustrystandard.com,html.]

Desktop distance learning (2000). [Retrieved March 19, 2002 from www.distance learning.com.html.]

Employee training: E-learning jumps 8 percent in organizations. (2001, November 6). *CIO* magazine. [Retrieved March 12, 2002, from www.CIO.com.html.]

Ehrmann, S. C.(2001). Improving outcomes of higher education. Why IT doesn't improve educational outcomes. Viewpoint Column in *Educasuse Review*. [Retrieved March 20, 2002, from www.tltgroup.org.html.]

Higher education e-learning market. (2001, December 18). Press Release: Eduventures releases study of higher education market, as subset of e-education. [Retrieved March 20, 2002, from www.e.learners.comhtml.]

Kounadis, T. (2001, July 17). *Opinion: E-learning and knowledge management at the crossroads*. [Retrieved March 11, 2002, from www.ospinion.com html.]

Long, H. B. (1987). *Education of adults in the United States*. London: Croom-Helm.

Log on for company training. (2000). Cited by Sarkey (2000). [Retrieved October 2, 2001, from www.businessweek.com.html.]

Mayor, T. (2001, January). E-learning: Does it make the grade? *CIO* magazine. [Retrieved March 19, 2002, from www. CIO.com/archives/html.]

Offerings. (2002, March 20). [Retrieved March 20, 2002 from www.e-learner .com.html.]

Overby, S. (2002, February 1). The world's biggest classroom. *CIO* magazine. [Retrieved March 20, 2002, from www.cio.com/archive/html.]

Redding, T.R., & Rotzien, J. (2001). A comparative analysis of pre-licensing insurance online learning with traditional classroom learning. In H. B. Long & Associates, *Self-directed learning and the information age* [CD-ROM]. Schaumburg, IL: Motorola University.

Sarkey, S. (2001, October 5). *Class report on websources*.

Stacy, O. (2000, September). *E-learning: September 29th, 2000*. [Retrieved March 20, 2002 from http://bctechnology.com/statitics/pstach-spt2900.html.]

Terry, L. (2000, April 6). On the job training. *Upside*. [Retrieved March 11, 2002, from www. Upside.com.html.]

Willison, F. (2001). *E-learning isn't all it's cracked up to be*. [Retrieved March 19, 2002, from www.oreilly.com./frank/elearning/html.]

About the Author

Huey B. Long, Ph.D., was a tenured faculty member at Florida State University, University of Georgia, and University of Oklahoma before retiring in 2002. In addition he served as a visiting professor at numerous international and American universities between 1975 and 2002. Dr. Long was appointed a professor in 1974 and also served as associate dean for research and graduate studies and director of graduate studies, College of Education, the University of Georgia. He was director of the Florida State University Urban Research Center and director of the Oklahoma Research Center for Continuing Professional and Higher Education, University of Oklahoma. Dr. Long has published more than seven hundred articles, books, and chapters.

Chapter 3

Becoming a More Self-Directed Learner

Why and How

Lucy M. and Paul J. Guglielmino

THIS CHAPTER IS DESIGNED TO ASSIST YOU in exploring an approach to learning that will support your e-learning success. The following questions will be addressed:

1. Why is becoming a self-directed learner important for your e-learning success?
2. What do you need to know about self-directed learning?
3. How can you develop your readiness for self-directed learning?
4. What learner support systems should you develop or ask for?

THE WHY OF SELF-DIRECTED LEARNING

You know some of them—the *innovators* who seem to be always one step ahead of everyone else: thinking, analyzing, identifying needs for new learning, and finding ways to meet them. In times of rapid change, learners like these acquire new skills, discover new techniques, and implement new processes; and they prosper. You also know the *clingers*—individuals who hold on to the old ways of doing things despite evidence that these approaches are no longer effective—the people who shy away from new technology and live defensively, not proactively.

Based on extensive research, the *innovators* are likely to be the highly self-directed learners. They are also more likely to be high performers on the job, to be at higher levels in their organizations, to be creative and entrepreneurial and to have greater life satisfaction. The *clingers* face a different scenario. Those who do not accept responsibility for identifying their own learning needs and making sure that these needs are addressed may find themselves to be obsolete (and possibly unemployed). (Curry, 1983; Durr, 1992; Guglielmino, 1994; Guglielmino & Guglielmino, 1981; Guglielmino & Klatt, 1994; Roberts, 1986).

Why is SDL readiness so important for e-learning? Because your best preparation for e-learning success is to enhance your readiness for self-direction in learning. In a national survey of trainers, professors, and learners involved in e-learning (Guglielmino & Guglielmino, 2001) two components of learner characteristics emerged as the most important for success in e-learning: readiness for self-direction in learning and technological readiness. Several studies have shown that the technical skills necessary for most e-learning are usually quickly mastered and very seldom, by themselves, reduce e-learning completion rates; therefore, enhancing your readiness for SDL becomes your most powerful avenue for e-learning success.

THE HOW OF SELF-DIRECTED LEARNING

Now that you have some idea as to why SDL is important for you as an e-learner, let's look at how you take advantage of that knowledge: What do you need to know about self-direction in learning?

Self-direction in learning has been described both as a process and as a psychological predisposition of the learner (Brockett & Hiemstra, 1991). SDL is a very natural process, and each person is a self-directed learner to some degree. The innovator and the clinger described earlier are two extremes of the spectrum. Similarly, learning situations offer varied levels of opportunity to exercise your self-direction.

The most frequently used definition of self-directed learning as a process was developed by Malcolm Knowles (1975), whose work provided a foundation for SDL in both educational and workplace contexts. He described SDL as a process in which the learner, with or without the help of others, identifies learning needs, defines learning goals, develops and implements a learning plan, and evaluates the learning gained. This cyclical process often results in the identification of new learning needs. The learners who are most likely to be successful in this process are those who have the highest levels of readiness for self-directed learning: a complex mixture of knowledge, skills, attitudes, and habits. Before proceeding, complete the exercise in Exhibit 3.1.

Exhibit 3.1. Action: Past SDL Projects

Write down at least three learning projects you have conducted in the past three years. Use the following criteria to define a learning project:

1. You took the major responsibility for the learning, especially in setting your goals for the learning and deciding which resources to use (books, videos, other individuals, classes, or experimental equipment, for example).
2. You spent at least seven hours on the learning project (not necessarily continuous). Include your planning time.

Write your projects in a grid like the one below:

Learning Project	**Hours Spent**	**Resources Used**

REFLECTION ON PAST SDL PROJECTS

What was your first reaction to being asked to name three self-learning projects? Which of the following reactions was closest to how you felt: "Have I done any?" "Suppose I can't think of any?" or "No problem, I can name more than three."?

If you had to think a while before listing your learning projects ("Have I done any?") or even had vague twinges of panic ("Suppose I can't think of any?"), you're completely normal. If "No problem" was your initial response, you are far more aware of yourself as a capable self-learner than the vast majority of adults are of themselves. A major study of self-learning projects (Tough, 1978) revealed that most adults are not very aware of themselves as continuing learners. Many people, in fact, are unable to list a single project they have conducted in the previous six months when first asked. Only after going through an extensive interview process could they recognize and describe their learning projects. Topics cover the range of human experience, from the most typical current learning project, mastering some aspect of computer technology or software, to learning for health reasons, leisure pursuits, home improvement, improvement of relationships, or for use in the workplace. Based just on the brief prompt provided by that list, you can probably now add many more projects to your list. Take a moment to think of some.

Were any of the learning projects you listed job-related? If so, are they listed on your resume?

Typically, many of the learning projects reported by adults are job-related, sometimes as many as half. You will not usually find learning projects conducted outside of formal educational institutions listed on résumés, however. This is easily understood in light of the fact that Tough found that most people vastly underestimate the value and extent of their learning projects.

How many self-directed learning projects would you guess the average adult conducts per year?

According to Tough's research, the average adult conducts eight learning projects per year. The average number of hours spent in learning projects in one year was 816, representing a range from 0 to 2,509. Average length of time spent on an individual learning project was 104 hours. Remember: The number of learning projects you listed in the previous exercise was based on an unprompted list. The figures cited from the Tough study are based on an in-depth interview, including examples of typical topics.

Once you begin thinking of things you have learned on your own and what others around you might have learned on their own, it becomes obvious that all of us are self-directed learners to some degree. Think for a moment about the people you know who seem to be always learning something new. Write down a few characteristics you would use to describe their attitudes, skills, and habits. The learners that you thought of are probably highly self-directed.

When a group of experts was asked to describe learners who would be likely to be successful in SDL, they arrived at this consensus:

> A highly self-directed learner is one who exhibits initiative, independence, and persistence in learning; one who accepts responsibility for his or her own learning and views problems as challenges, not obstacles; one who is capable of self-discipline and has a high degree of curiosity; one who has a strong desire to learn or change and is self-confident; one who is able to use basic study skills, organize his or her time, set an appropriate pace for learning, and develop a plan for completing work; one who enjoys learning and has a tendency to be goal-oriented. (Guglielmino, 1977–78, p. 73)

The definition suggests a variety of knowledge, attitudes, skills, and habits that are involved in readiness for self-directed learning. How can you develop these to enhance your readiness for self-directed learning?

How can you develop your readiness for self-directed learning? Now that we have looked at the past and present, we need to consider the future.

Knowledge of SDL

The first step in improving your readiness for SDL is gaining an understanding of self-direction in learning, which you have already begun by reading this chapter. It is important to realize that SDL is a very natural way of learning and that you can consciously improve your SDL readiness through your efforts and experiences.

Self-Knowledge

Readiness for self-directed learning requires self-knowledge: an understanding of yourself as a learner based on an honest appraisal. To assist your analysis of yourself as a learner, you can use any of the following:

- Learning style assessments to determine your preferred ways of taking in and processing information (see www.vark-learn.com/english/index.asp)
- Multiple intelligences inventories to determine your learning strengths (see www.multi-intell.com/mi_overview.htm), or
- The Learning Preference Assessment (Guglielmino & Guglielmino, 1991) to assess your current level of readiness for self-directed learning (see www.guglielmino734.com)

Answer the questions in Exhibit 3.2 after trying one of the assessments mentioned above.

Exhibit 3.2. Action and Reflection: Self as Learner

Develop a learning profile for yourself:

1. How do you usually prefer to take in information? Are you a visual, aural, kinesthetic, or interactive learner?

Exhibit 3.2. Action and Reflection: Self as Learner, Cont'd

2. What are your strongest intelligences?

3. How strong is your readiness for SDL?

4. What are some adaptations you might use if you need to be involved in a learning situation that does not match your preferred learning styles or your stronger intelligences?

SDL Attitudes

Some attitudes that support SDL are easier to develop than others. In this chapter, we will focus on only a few. One of the most fundamental is *confidence in yourself as a competent, effective learner.* Seeing yourself as a "can-do" learner leads you to take the initiative in learning. Thinking back over the number of things you have learned on your own that you wrote down in Exhibit 3.1 and recognizing that much of your most important learning has been self-learning should provide a strong base for this attitude.

Closely related to this attitude are two others: *accepting responsibility for your own learning* and *viewing problems as challenges rather than obstacles*. The successful self-directed learner believes that the primary responsibility for learning belongs to the learner, not the instructor, professor, or trainer. You are the one who must recognize your own needs for learning and take the responsibility for making it happen, regardless of the course design, other inviting activities, unforeseen occurrences—all the distractions that are used by some as an excuse for avoiding, postponing, or giving up on a learning project.

Creativity and *independence in learning* are also crucial in many of the well-designed e-learning settings, settings that require analysis, independent work, and the creation of products that must combine theory and practice. If you are accustomed to very structured learning settings built around memorization and following exact directions, you may need a bit of time to adjust to assignments requiring more creativity and independence, but don't hesitate to ask questions and compare notes with other learners.

A *willingness to seek help* also facilitates self-directed learning. The idea of the self-directed learner as a lone wolf struggling to find answers in isolation is a myth. An effective self-directed learner uses all the tools available, then invents those that are not.

Individuals who are reluctant to "show their ignorance" by asking questions, seeking clarification, or seeking out expert advice handicap themselves in terms of learning progress. Those who are willing to ask for help reduce the time involved in responding to problems and challenges and avoid frustration that can lead to poor completion rates.

Another helpful attitude is *valuing your own learning*—a belief in the importance of learning achieved on your own. In most of your experiences in our formal educational system, you have had an instructor who tells you what to learn, how to learn it, and when you will be tested on it and who then gives you a grade to let you know how well you met the expectations imposed on you. This type of experience naturally leads us to devalue the learning achieved outside of formal classroom situations. Learners soon get the idea that learning that takes place outside of a classroom or a training room doesn't count. The expansion of knowledge in the information age makes this concept not only foolish, but potentially damaging. New challenges and obstacles now arise daily, and if individuals wait for someone else to tell them what to learn, they and their organizations will lag behind instead of leading. Check your own attitudes about learning in Exhibit 3.3.

Exhibit 3.3. Action and Behavior: Attitudes

Adopt your attitudes toward learning on your own as a continuous self-improvement project. Become more aware of the messages you send yourself about yourself as a learner and consciously monitor your self-talk to develop your SDL attitudes. Examine your thoughts, attitudes, and your self-talk when engaged in learning by using the following questions:

- Do I feel capable of finding a way to learn almost anything I might need to learn?
- Do I usually take the initiative in learning, or do I wait for someone to tell me what needs to be learned and how and when it will be learned?
- Am I focused on gaining the information and skills, or just meeting the requirements of a class or training session?
- When problems and barriers occur, do I feel overburdened or defeated, or do I remind myself that overcoming obstacles is just a natural part of the learning process and quickly begin to mentally play with ways of meeting the challenge and accomplishing my learning goal? Does my self-talk sound more like "What if I tried it this way?" than "If only this hadn't happened!"?
- Am I willing to admit that I need help sometimes and seek it from learning facilitators, experts, friends, co-learners?
- Am I proud of what I learn on my own? Do I acknowledge my learning accomplishments and gain satisfaction from them?

Once you have thought through the questions, identify areas that you want to target for improvement and design a plan for addressing them (see the information on developing a learning plan in the next section of this chapter).

SDL Skills and Habits

Logically, basic academic skills are an important part of readiness for e-learning, especially reading skills. Depending on the instructional design, writing skills can also be critical. Self-directed learners are also usually skilled at identifying and analyzing their learning needs. Key skills related to meeting these learning needs include the ability to set learning goals, develop a learning plan, identify resources for learning (both human and material), implement the learning, and evaluate the learning. Time management skills and document or report preparation skills support this process as well.

Both habits of thought and habits of action can provide vital support for SDL. Highly self-directed learners have a high level of curiosity and a strong desire to learn, so they are continually thinking. They habitually analyze their own learning processes and learning outcomes, engaging in a process called *meta-learning.* In other words, they are in the habit of observing and analyzing things in a search for new insights, new meaning, new questions. A part of this reflection is environmental scanning, an ongoing, active awareness of changes in the environment and their possible implications, including possible needs for new learning.

One of the most important habits of the successful self-directed learner is the habit of persistence—the refusal to be deterred from reaching a goal because of problems, boredom, or other factors or events that might derail a less determined learner. Habits such as systematic planning, productive organization of learning media and materials, and completing tasks within the time scheduled can streamline and anchor effective e-learning.

SDL SKILLS AND HABITS

Obviously, some of the SDL skills and habits develop over long time spans and could not be adequately addressed in this chapter. We will focus on a few brief guidelines and planning tools, which, if used regularly, can help to develop SDL skills and habits.

Organize

Analyze each new learning situation to maximize your gain and the gain for your organization. Assess what will be most useful to you, plan an approach to learning, and set a timetable. Two tools that could be helpful to you in this process are learning contracts and time/task calendars.

A *time/task calendar* can be extremely useful in any learning situation. It simply requires you to look at the task before you, break it into manageable segments, and commit to logical deadlines for completing each part of the task. You might want to keep one copy with your learning materials, but be sure to transfer the deadlines to whatever type of daily calendar you use. When you do this, you are creating a type of tickler file that will help you to meet your deadlines.

In less structured e-learning situations, or for major projects within a learning situation, you may want to use a *learning plan* or *learning contract*. A learning contract simply lays out, in a very brief and easy-to-read format, four essential components of your learning: your specific objectives, your learning process and resources, a target date, and an evaluation standard. To develop a learning plan, ask yourself four questions:

1. "What do I need to know or be able to do?" Your answer becomes your learning objective.
2. "What steps will I take to learn this and what resources will I use?" Your list may include a variety of resources, both human and material.
3. "When will I complete this?" A target date for completion of the learning objective facilitates your planning.
4. "What will my evaluation standard be?" It is important to decide from the beginning how you will measure your success. Is total mastery required, or just a working knowledge?

For more detailed information on learning contracts, see Knowles (1977) and Guglielmino and Guglielmino (1991, 1999).

Use Support Systems

Get in the habit of using learner support systems or developing your own. Check the online help options, ask a friend or colleague with expertise, consult a learning resource center facilitator, if available, and explore mentoring options.

Seek Appropriate Delivery Systems—or Adapt!

Regularly apply your new knowledge of yourself as a learner to choose an e-learning delivery option that you believe you can be successful with. Do you need an onsite facilitator? Would you prefer learning that is totally online? Do you function better in audio-based learning platforms? Seek appropriate learning environments when the choices are available, and adapt your approach when they are not.

All learning options offer varied levels of opportunity for self-direction, but the highly self-directed learner is better equipped to gain from any learning experience.

SUMMARY

Enhancing Your Readiness for
Self-Direction in Learning: The Short List

Become a more ACTIVE learner:

- **A**ssess yourself as a learner. Become more aware of your preferred learning styles, your strongest intelligences, and your SDL KASH (Knowledge Attitudes Skills Habit).
- **C**ontemplate your previous SDL projects. Think about what you learned and how you learned it. Recall the problems or challenges and how you overcame them. Remember the feeling of satisfaction you gained from your learning.
- **T**ake time to think about all the possible resources for SDL. Depending on the type of learning you are doing, your list

may include books, articles, manuals, computer databases, Internet Web sites, human experts, experiments, or a variety of other resources.

- **I**nvestigate and practice using tools that can support and streamline your SDL, such as learning contracts and time/task calendars.
- **V**alue and celebrate your learning.
- **E**valuate and reflect continually, monitoring the accomplishment of your learning goals and identifying new needs for learning.

References

For all references cited in this chapter, see www.guglielmino734.com/newpage3.htm.

About the Authors

Dr. Lucy Guglielmino is currently professor of adult and community education at Florida Atlantic University in Boca Raton, Florida. Her doctorate is in adult education from the University of Georgia (1977). Dr. Guglielmino is best known for her development of the *Self-Directed Learning Readiness Scale* (with a self-scoring form known as the *Learning Preference Assessment*). The *SDLRS* has been translated into twelve languages and used in more than three dozen countries. In addition, Dr. Guglielmino has authored or co-authored more than ninety books, chapters, articles, monographs, and other written materials on various aspects of adult learning, training, and development. She is listed in many honoraries, including *Notable American Women*, *Who's Who in America*, and *Who's Who in the World*.

Dr. Paul Guglielmino is an associate professor of management at Florida Atlantic University. He teaches undergraduate and graduate level courses in the area of general management, entrepreneurship, and new business formation. In 1998, Dr. Guglielmino was selected University Distinguished Teacher of the Year at Florida Atlantic University. He has served as an advisory board member at Walt Disney World in Orlando and has consulted with companies such as Disney, Motorola, AT&T, Johnson & Johnson, and Medtronic. Dr. Guglielmino is a member of the Academy of Management and a past member of the Academy of International Business. He has published more than thirty academic articles and book chapters. His Web site address is www.guglielmino734.com.

Chapter 4

How to Prepare to Attend a Synchronous E-Learning Course

Bill Knapp

ATTENDING A SYNCHRONOUS OR LIVE E-LEARNING COURSE is much like attending a course in another city. As you prepare to attend, you may consider what you need to bring, how you will travel to the site, and your feelings about the trip. If this is the first time you are making a trip out of state, you may wonder about items such as refreshments for the trip, appropriate clothing, whether to bring reading materials, whether you remembered your registration confirmations, and whether you have created a viable travel schedule. You may also notify people at work or home that you will be gone and when you will return. The trip may include travel by commercial airline and the course site may be in a location you have never visited. Some people react to these situations as exciting challenges, while others experience anxiety. One way to improve your feelings of confidence and your success in the course is by thoroughly planning your trip and preparing yourself. Each step in this process has an equivalent in a synchronous or live e-learning course. In this chapter, you will explore how to prepare for your first synchronous journey to ensure a successful experience. This preparation is divided into four major groups: mindset, course content, technology, and the environment of synchronous courses.

In the previous chapter on self-directed learning, the concept of our learning styles and readiness for self-directed learning was discussed. In this chapter you will explore specific actions you may take to prepare for a successful journey into synchronous course delivery.

This chapter is intended for people who are about to join their first synchronous course. It may also be of benefit to presenters and organizers of courses as a guideline for preparing new users. All learners—corporate, academic, and consumer—will benefit from the recommendations presented. At key points in the chapter, checklists are included. These checklists may be used as quick reference guides when you are performing the steps identified. Let's take a moment to define a few key terms.

In this chapter, *facilitator* refers to the person teaching or leading the course. A synchronous course may have one or multiple facilitators. *Participants* are the people attending the course sessions. On occasion a course may include presentations by subject-matter experts, also know as SMEs. Any software required to attend a synchronous session will be referred to as the *participant software*. Many synchronous software systems provide separate software for the course facilitator. By this time you are probably wondering what *synchronous* means. The *American Heritage Dictionary* defines *synchronous* as "moving or occurring at the same time." This is different from *asynchronous*, which means "to occur at different times." What has this to do with attending a course? Most e-learning courses or computer-based training (CBT) courses are asynchronous, in that the person who created the course is not in the course at the same time as the persons attending the course. In a synchronous course, also known as a live e-learning event, the participants and the facilitator(s) are in the course at the exact same time. This is why it is called "live." You may interact with the facilitator, asking questions and receiving answers just like you would in a classroom-based course (c-learning). One attends synchronous courses by connecting to a site on the Internet (or intranet) and joining a virtual classroom online.

This chapter describes the use of software functionality commonly found in synchronous software packages. The names of these functions and the buttons or menu choices in your course may vary from those used in this text. Two of the most popular software vendors, Centra and Interwise, require a software program be installed on the participants' computers prior to attending live sessions. If you are responsible for the installation of the course software, basic computer skills and knowledge of Microsoft Windows is recommended in order to complete the technology steps identified in this chapter. Some of the technology installation steps may have been completed by your company's or school's IT department. Exhibit 4.1 provides you with Web addresses of some of the major vendors.

Exhibit 4.1. Synchronous Software Vendor Web Sites

Centra: www.centra.com
Interwise: www.interwise.com
Mentergy: www.montergy.com
Placeware: www.placeware.com
WebEx: www.webex.com

PREPARATION STEPS

One way to approach this journey is to divide the trip into lists of easily accomplished steps. For a synchronous course there are four major groups: mindset, course content, technology, and the environment. *Mindset* is how you approach the course. If you are afraid of the technology, are ill prepared, or do not look for ways to participate, you greatly reduce your chances of having a positive experience. This is true whether you are on a vacation or attending a classroom or synchronous session. *Course content* covers two areas: prework and content delivered in the live session. *Technology* examines the software and hardware involved in connecting to a synchronous course. *Environment* is the characteristics of the location from which you will attend the course. Preparation in these four areas should be reviewed each time you attend a course provided by a different company or school. When attending a series of sessions or courses from the same source, many of the steps do not need to be repeated. At the end of this chapter, a separate checklist is provided that identifies those items that you should do each time you attend a session in a series of synchronous sessions. Let's begin by examining techniques you may employ to prepare your mindset.

Mindset

There are two aspects of mindset that affect success in a synchronous session: your comfort with the technology and your attitude toward learning. Both of these impact the way you feel about the first and possibly subsequent sessions. This can be broken down into a number of facets:

- How you feel about attending online
- How you intend to participate, and
- Your ability to feel connected with others in the session

It is normal to feel isolated or disconnected from the facilitator and classmates in a synchronous session. After all, you cannot see them or hear everyone in the course. You do not have a sense of their reactions to you or to the material being presented. In most synchronous sessions you will hear the facilitator talking, and on occasion you may hear a classmate ask or answer a question. So what can you do to deal with these differences in experience?

The software you will be using to connect to the course provides a variety of ways to interact with the facilitator and others in the course. You will have the ability to signal the facilitator that you have a question by clicking on a "raise hand" button, send questions by voice or text message, and exchange text messages with others in the course. Being familiar with the capabilities of the software and the function of each button will help you feel comfortable attending the course. Most software vendors offer free courses on their

Web sites that allow you to "play" with the user interface and learn how it works before attending your first course session. This is a great way to become comfortable with the software, reducing your fear of the technology. Be sure to validate with your course provider which software will be used for your course before going to a vendor's Web site.

One of the features of taking a trip that makes the experience fun is the activities. These may be visiting a historical site, enjoying fishing or boating, or meeting new people. Each of these features is fun because you participate in the activity. Well-designed synchronous courses contain many opportunities to participate.

Opportunities to Participate

- Respond to surveys
- Answer review questions
- Capture brainstormed ideas on a whiteboard
- Participate in online discussions

However, if you choose to ignore these opportunities you will feel isolated from the course and it will no longer be fun. Other ways you may connect to people in the course is to create a digital photo of yourself in JPG or GIF format and share it with others in the course. Some courses have a Web site associated with the course that allows you to easily create a personal Web page containing your picture, a brief description of yourself, and a list of your interests. These techniques are part of the steps you may take to build virtual relationships with your facilitator and classmates.

In a classroom course there are expectations and ground rules as to how you are to interact with the facilitator and your classmates. These include topics such as the attendance policy, when assignments are due, timing of breaks, and how to signal that you wish to ask a question. In a synchronous course similar guidelines exist.

Live E-Learning Session Etiquette

- Close all other applications, except the applications you will be using for this session:
  - Do not communicate with others by instant messenger or e-mail.
  - Do not work on other activities while attending the course.
- Dialogue is important:
  - Speak slowly.
  - Ask for permission to speak by "raising your hand."
  - Pause after you have spoken to allow time for the response—there will be a slight delay in the audio streaming.
- Sending questions:
  - You may "raise your hand" to verbally ask a question.
  - Use the chat capability to type your question.
  - Follow the facilitator's guidelines as to when to ask questions, whether during the presentation or at the end of a section.

Before attending your first session, check the communications from the facilitator for these guidelines. If they are not included in the registration communications or prework, they may be part of the introduction to the first session. Now that we have completed examining how to prepare your mindset for your synchronous journey, let's examine the next section: content.

Content

The course content is the main reason for attending a synchronous session. Content can be divided into three areas: course prework, content delivered in the live session, and individual assignments. One way to approach synchronous courses is to view them as an opportunity to validate your understanding of the content. If you know nothing about the course content, it is even more important to plan your approach to it. Unlike a classroom course in which the course session takes place with the facilitator present, in a synchronous course a large portion of the course time takes place away from the facilitator, doing reading, completing other assignments, and interacting with classmates through tools such as bulletin boards. It is your responsibility to identify and complete prework assignments before the live session. This is especially import if the assignments are reading and posting personal information such as your picture to a Web site. You certainly don't want to be the only one who has not shared his or her picture at the start of the course!

While completing the reading assignments, identify your knowledge gaps and create a list of questions to ask the facilitator during a live session. This helps you prepare your mindset for the course and maximizes the learning you may achieve. Print the questions and have them available during the session. If available, review the content outline or session topics and organize your questions to match the sequence of the session presentations. This technique will help you organize your thoughts while relating the content to knowledge you already have. As the questions are answered, capture the answers on your list. Another technique is to create your personal course objectives—identifying what you would like to achieve by attending the course. This may be simply an awareness of the topic or deep technical knowledge leading to a certification. Now that we have completed the discussion of course content, let's examine the technology aspect of attending a synchronous course.

Technology

When facilitators organize classroom courses, they make arrangements for the meeting room, printing of course materials, and use of audiovisual equipment. The selection of synchronous software, creation of electronic versions of the materials, and the scheduling of the session are the synchronous equivalent. For classroom courses, you travel to the course site and select a seat in the room to view the presentation. In a synchronous session, traveling to the course is accomplished through use of the Internet connection. You can think of your computer running the participant software as your own personal classroom. Your boarding pass and photo ID are your login and password, while your seat in the course is the view provided by the participant software running on your computer. Let's examine methods to ensure that you are able to connect to the course and take full advantage of the software's features.

Any time you are going to use your computer in a new way there are three aspects you must consider: hardware, software, and testing.

The *hardware* required for attending a synchronous session is generally the standard components found in most computers manufactured in the previous two years. This includes a sound card, speakers or a headset, and a modem. If your computer does not have a sound card, you will not be able to hear the course presentations and interactions with the facilitator. Installing a sound card may be a complex task; it is recommended that you have a professional perform the installation.

If your computer does not have a modem to connect you to the Internet, a modem may be easily added. External modems are available that simply plug into the computer's serial port. Your computer owner's manual clearly identifies the location of this port. The faster the speed of the modem, the better the performance will be of the participant software. The type and speed of your Internet service also impacts performance. Internet access may be provided by dial-up through a phone line, by a high-speed connection such as cable modem, or by an office LAN. If you are connecting via dial-up, the performance of the software may be impaired, especially if you have a slow connection at a rate below 56K. In some cases, you may not be able to use functionality such as application sharing or live video. Therefore, always use the fastest connection possible when attending a synchronous course. See Exhibit 4.2 for a discussion of connection speeds.

Exhibit 4.2. Connection Speeds

The unit of measure for connection speed, baud, is measured in kilobytes and megabytes (1,024 kilobytes). A low baud rate of 24K is normally not powerful enough to handle complex graphics such as live video. Higher speeds such as normally provided by an office LAN or cable modem support the needs of a synchronous course. However, keep in mind that you may be sharing the connection with others. For example, at lunch time in an office there may be many people using the same Internet connection. This is much like driving on an expressway. At 3 A.M. you may have the entire road to yourself, but at rush hour you share the road with many drivers and, depending on the volume of traffic, your speed may be slowed down to a crawl. This is identical for Internet access, that is, the total traffic on the connection impacts the individual response. At worst case, you receive an error such as "page not available" before receiving the screen you are requesting. If your connection is very slow, this error may be a "time out error" rather than an error caused by the Internet site being down or an incorrect address. Time out errors occur when your request for connection or data from a Web site does not respond within the time specified in connection settings. For example, your browser can be set to cancel the request if it does not respond within one minute. Your Internet service provider may also have time out settings that effect your connection. These exist to reduce the time spent searching for sites that do not exist or ones for which you have made a typing error in specifying the URL.

One item that is not generally included with most computers is a microphone for speaking over the Internet. Many of the popular synchronous software packages now support voice-over IP technology or VOI. This capability allows the facilitator and participants to speak to one another without using a telephone. The most practical microphone for this purpose is one that is built into a headset. Not having to lean over or hold a microphone leaves your hands free to operate the software. Headset microphones are designed to pick up sound originating from a direct, close-by location, while microphones on a stand will pick up much more background noise. A headset is also preferred if you will be attending the course where background noise would make it difficult to hear your speakers. The headset allows you to listen without disturbing others in the same room. Headsets generally have two plugs on the end of the wire, one for the headset jack on your computer and the second for the microphone jack. Make sure that both are plugged into the correct ports before starting the synchronous software. This completes the hardware portion; the next step is the installation of the participant software.

The installation of the participant *software* is very easy to complete. The first step is to review the instructions from the course organizers. Generally the instructions tell you to do one of three things: nothing (that is, no software installation required), install from a web address, or install from a supplied disk (floppy or CD-ROM). Review the instructions provided by the course organizer and determine which one of these choices applies. If the instructions specify software to be installed, check to see if detailed instructions are provided. If the installation is from a website, the instructions are probably on the site. The following is a checklist for installing software:

- Print out instructions.
- Record responses to configuration questions.
- Create screen captures of key information.
- Fully document any errors.

The first step is to be completed if the instructions were not provided in a written form. Having a paper copy allows you to take notes on the instructions. If you have a problem, you may document exactly where in the process the error occurred. Often, you will be asked to supply information about your computer or personal details. Typical questions you may be asked are

- Installation directory
- Your name
- Your company/school

- User ID
- Password
- Server address (URL)

The installation directory is the location on your computer's hard disk drive where the software will be placed; always accept the default directory path. The next two fields are obvious, your name and company. If you are not employed, leave the company field blank. The user ID, also called your "login," is a unique name used by the software to identify you in the registration and attendance records. The login is also used to validate who you are when you join the course session. Most schools or companies use a combination of your first and last names, such as first letter of your first name and your full last name. It is very important that you record the user ID in a safe place. In some cases, you will be informed of your user ID and password in the registration confirmation. The password is the second part of the login credentials and is required to join the course. If a password is not supplied, you will be prompted to enter a combination of letters and numbers. *Note:* Some software packages use case-sensitive passwords. In this case be sure to record you password exactly as you typed it, including any capitalization used.

Some software may also ask for the address of the server or campus. This is the URL that you enter in your Internet browser when connecting to the session. This address should be included with your registration confirmation or other communications from the course supplier. If you are uncertain as to the correct URL, contact the supplier prior to installing the software. If you do not have this information you will not be able to connect to the course. Once you have a printed copy of the instructions and have identified the information listed, you are ready to install the software.

As the installation program is running, keep track of any error messages received, write down answers you provide to questions or requests for data, and note any phone numbers of other information provided for you to contact if you have a problem. One effective way to document settings and error messages is to create screen captures. While holding down the Alt key on your keyboard, press the Print Screen key. A copy of the screen is placed in the paste buffer. To save the copy, open a paint package such as MSPaint or any word processing program and paste the image by holding down the Ctrl key and pressing the letter "V." A copy of the screen is now displayed in the program; use the File: Save command to save this copy. You may also print a copy and place it with the installation notes. Once the software is installed, the next step is to test the software and any new hardware.

Testing may be broken down into the following areas for synchronous courses:

- Audio tuning
- Microphone tuning
- Participant software functionality
- Connectivity

Audio and microphone tuning validates that they are working properly and are set to comfortable levels. To test them, you may use the sound recorder installed with Microsoft Windows or a similar program. Some participant software programs have an audio tuner built into the installation process. This tuner will allow you to play and record sounds to adjust the audio levels to a comfortable setting.

Sound Recorder

To access the Sound Recorder, go to the Start menu and select Programs, then Accessories, then Entertainment. The Sound Recorder should be in the Entertainment menu. Click on Sound Recorder to start the program. If the program is not in the Entertainment menu on your computer, check other menus such as Multimedia. Sound Recorder is an electronic version of a cassette player. The program has, starting from the bottom left edge of the screen, buttons for rewind, fast forward, play, record, and stop. Go ahead and click on the Record button to validate that the microphone is OK and works without error. After recording a few sentences, press the Stop button and then Play. You should hear the sentences you recorded. If the volume is too low, use your computer's volume control settings to adjust the microphone level and speaker level. These are accessible by clicking on the Speaker icon located in the Start menu bar near the far right end.

Troubleshooting

If your headset or microphone does not work, there are a few things that you may do to troubleshoot the problem. First, validate that the levels for both are set at least midway in the slider bars. Second, check that the headset plugs are in the correct ports and fully seated. Third, check whether there is a volume control on the headset or on its wire and set the control to halfway. Also, check whether there is a switch for the microphone. Fourth, some computers also have a hardware control near the place where the headset connects. There may be an on/off switch and a volume control. If there is, validate that the headset is on and the volume is set to halfway. If these steps do not solve the problem, seek professional help from your company's help desk or your local computer store.

Next, if you installed the participant software, let's test that it is functioning properly. Most course providers include a phone number and procedure to validate your software installation and test your connectivity to the synchronous server. Follow their instructions to perform the test. The following is an example of testing an installation of Interwise 4.x participant software:

1. Launch your Internet browser software, such as Internet Explorer.
2. Enter the URL supplied by the course provider for the campus or the test site URL if a separate one is provided.
3. Log in to the campus using your user ID and password.

4. Connect to a test or sample course.
5. The participant software should launch and you will be asked if you wish to download the course materials. Click on "yes" to accept the materials. If each of these steps was completed without error messages being displayed, you have successfully completed the testing.
6. Now is a good time to add the course site address to your browser favorites. This will save you time later when you connect to the course.

This list was typical of the steps required to connect to most synchronous software. If you were not successful installing or testing the connection, let's examine how to deal with errors you may receive. Handling errors is often a three-step process:

1. Document the error.
2. Analyze the error.
3. Take corrective action.

In some cases such as "invalid user ID or password," you need to refer to your notes to validate that you did not make a typing error. In other cases, you may need to contact the course provider to have their help desk assist with troubleshooting the problem. Before contacting anyone, document the error you are receiving by making a screen capture of the error message and writing down where in the process the error occurred. When you call a help desk, have the documentation ready and be prepared to test the software with the help desk person. In terms of your mindset when speaking with a help desk person, be patient. The person cannot see your computer screen and must rely on you accurately describing the problem in order to help you. Also, don't act defensive; describe all actions before the error occurred, even if you feel they were not important. Sometimes other software running on your computer may interfere with the participant software or its connection to the synchronous server. Also, refer to the discussion earlier in this chapter regarding connection speed. Whenever you are using the Internet, your connection speed has a great impact on the error messages you receive. Now that your computer is ready for the course, let's examine your work environment.

Environment

The work environment is the physical space you will connect from. This includes your desk, the room, and the proximity of others. This environment may be perfect for attending a synchronous course or it may have characteristics that interfere with your ability to focus on the course content. For example, if there are others in the room and the noise level is high, this may not be the best place for attending the course. Think of your location as if entering a physical classroom. Is this the best environment to attend the course or should you move to a quieter location? Let's evaluate a location by using the checklist in Exhibit 4.3.

Exhibit 4.3. Environmental Checklist

- ☐ Quiet—level of background noise
- ☐ Distraction-Free—no ringing phones or others talking
- ☐ Private—comfortable to talk to others online
- ☐ Space—room for computer, documentation, and taking notes
- ☐ Power for the computer
- ☐ Internet connection
- ☐ Comfortable environment
- ☐ Lighting—appropriate for computer use

As indicated by the items on the checklist, the location of your computer while you attend a synchronous course is very similar in characteristics to locations for a classroom course. If you are connecting at work, a private office or conference room is the best location. It is very difficult to attend from an open space such as an office cubicle. The number one complaint of attendees in synchronous courses is distractions during the session. Now that you have selected a location, let's examine the organization of your work area.

In addition to your computer, have a pad of paper to take notes, a Post-it pad to jot down temporary information such as a person's nickname, writing instruments, and something to drink. You should also have the connection information and the list of questions you created when you reviewed the course content and reading assignments. Another consideration in arranging your environment is the people who will be around you while you are attending the course. Inform people that you are attending a live course and request that you not be disturbed. Before the course date, share the course schedule with your supervisor or others who will be in the area. It is important that they understand what you are doing and that it requires your full attention during the scheduled time. Schedule your day around the session to allow time to prepare for the first session—at least one hour—and time to set up and begin the connection process about half an hour before the start time. You may even place a sign on the room door: "Live Training Session in Progress." This completes your examination of the steps you may take to optimize your first synchronous course experience. Now let's examine steps to take within an hour of the start of the first course session.

ONE HOUR BEFORE START TIME

This list is numbered sequentially because the steps should be performed in a certain sequence. If you do all of these steps, it will take about an hour, but the benefit is that you will be relaxed, in the right mindset, and ready to participate in the course.

1. Gather course reference materials.
2. Check for additional facilitator communications.
3. Review your list of questions.
4. Have a digital photo of yourself available on your computer.
5. Set up in the location from which you will attend the course.
6. Close other applications running on your computer.
7. Log on to the course.
8. Launch a word processor for spelling checks.

About an hour before the first session begins, review your registration confirmation and other communications to ensure that you know how to connect to the course. Also, take out your list of questions and any printouts of course schedule or agenda and facilitator communications. Review the questions, session topic, and guidelines for live sessions established by the facilitator. This will help you focus on the purpose of the session. If guidelines are not provided, add a note to your list of questions and wait to see if they are covered by the facilitator in the first session. If not, then at the end of the session ask how questions will be handled: at the end of each presentation, at the end of a major concept, or at any time during the session.

If the course has a Web site or portal, it is a good habit to check for additional communications from the facilitator. Also, check for assignments that are to be completed prior to the live session and verify that you have completed the assignments! Also have a digital photo of yourself available if you did not post one to a course Web site.

If you are attending the course from a different room, move to the room and set up your computer and materials. Half an hour prior to the live session, turn off e-mail, instant messaging, and any programs that use an Internet connection. These consume bandwidth of your Internet connection and may interfere with the participant software; at the very least they are a distraction during the course session. You should also turn off mobile phones and beepers, close the room door, and place a sign on the door indicating that a training session is taking place in the room. Now is a good time to verify that your headset is connecting properly and that the microphone is functioning. You may use the test procedure listed above to verify audio tuning. Next, log in to the course site and verify that the course is listed. *Note:* You may not be able to launch the course until fifteen minutes before the scheduled start time. As soon as the course is available, launch the course, and, if prompted, download the course presentation. You are now fully prepared to attend your first live synchronous session.

This was a long, detailed process in which you examined many things you may do to improve your preparation for the course content, your comfort level with the technology, and the setup and testing of your computer. It is not necessary to do each of these items for subsequent sessions in the same course. Following is a checklist for attending the balance of the sessions in one course.

Before Subsequent Sessions

1. Complete course assignments.
2. Update your list of questions.
3. Review session objectives.
4. Gather course reference materials.
5. Check for additional facilitator communications.
6. Set up in the location from which you will attend the course.
7. Close other applications.
8. Log on to the course.
9. Launch a word processor for spelling checks.

How is this different from attending your first session? The mindset activities are a one-time event and you should feel comfortable with the technology after the first session. The content is different in each session, and your preparation of questions and completion of assignments is an activity you should do before each session. All of the technology preparation should have been completed for the first session and does not need to be repeated unless you had problems.

SUMMARY

The material in this chapter completed our examination of preparing to attend a synchronous course. When you attend the course you will feel confident because you have planned your trip and thoroughly prepared yourself. In this chapter, you explored four major aspects of synchronous courses: mindset, course content, technology, and the environment.

In the next chapter, you will examine how to maximize the benefits received when attending a synchronous course.

About the Author

Bill Knapp is a senior manager in the Learning Edge Group in Deloitte Consulting and is responsible for global virtual learning infrastructure. In this role he is responsible for the deployment of internally developed distance learning courses, supporting infrastructure, and technical training of distance learning instructors. During his career, he has developed a wide range of training materials for synchronous courses, asynchronous learning content, self-study workbooks, multimedia presentations, live action videos, and classroom-based courses. At Deloitte he has developed and delivered courses globally, both in person and over the Internet, addressing the local needs of learners in countries such as Japan, China, Singapore, Holland, Germany, Italy, and the United States.

Knapp has more than twenty-five years experience as a professional educator, delivering courses in both the public and private sectors. During his career he has specialized in technology training, delivering topics such as computer-aided drafting, robotics, and ERP solutions.

Chapter 5

How to Attend a Synchronous E-Learning Course

Bill Knapp

IN CHAPTER 4 WE EXAMINED how attending a synchronous or live e-learning course is much like attending a classroom course in another city. There are things you must do to prepare for your trip to the course site to ensure that you arrive on time in the correct location. In this chapter you will explore things to do that will increase the likelihood of having a positive and fun experience while attending the course. You will also examine capabilities of the synchronous software that allow you to do many of the same activities as in a classroom course and strategies to receive the most benefit from the time you are online. Let's take a moment to review a few definitions associated with synchronous courses. If you just read Chapter 4, skip this portion and skip the section under the heading: One Hour Before Course Start Time and go directly to the heading: Attending the Course to learn what to do now that you have arrived in the live synchronous course.

If you have not read Chapter 4, the next few paragraphs will summarize the key concepts covered there. People who are about to join their first synchronous course will benefit from the comparison between classroom and synchronous courses. This chapter may also be of benefit to facilitators and organizers of courses as a guideline for preparing new users. All learners—corporate, academic, and consumer—will benefit from the recommendations presented.

At key points in the chapter, checklists are included. These checklists may be used as quick reference guides when you are performing the steps identified. Let's take a moment to define a few key terms.

The *American Heritage Dictionary* defines *synchronous* as "moving or occurring at the same time." Synchronous courses can then be defined as an online learning event that is lead by a facilitator at a scheduled time and date. There are a number of ways in which classroom and synchronous courses are similar:

- Both are led by a facilitator.
- There are other participants in the course.
- The course takes place at a specific time in a set location.

The difference between classroom and synchronous is that in a classroom course everyone is in the same location, while in a synchronous course people may be attending from different locations anywhere in the world. One attends synchronous courses by connecting to a site on the Internet (or an intranet) and joining a virtual classroom online.

In this chapter, *facilitator* refers to the person teaching or leading the course. A synchronous course may have one or multiple facilitators. *Participants* are the people attending the course. On occasion a course may include presentations by subject-matter experts, also known as SMEs. Any software required to attend a synchronous course will be referred to as the *participant software*. Many synchronous software systems provide separate software for the course facilitator. Let's take a moment to review the steps you should take, starting one hour prior to the scheduled start of the synchronous course. These steps were covered in some detail in Chapter 4. If you just read Chapter 4, skip to the header Attending the Course to learn what to do now that you have arrived in the live course.

ONE HOUR BEFORE START TIME

This list is numbered sequentially because the steps should be performed in a certain sequence. If you do all of these steps, it will take about an hour, but the benefit is that you will be relaxed, in the right mindset, and ready to participate in the course.

1. Gather course reference materials.
2. Check for additional facilitator communications.
3. Review your list of questions.
4. Have a digital photo of yourself available on your computer.
5. Set up in the location from which you will attend the course.
6. Close other applications running on your computer.
7. Log on to the course.
8. Launch a word processor for spelling checks.

ATTENDING THE COURSE

This chapter describes the use of software functionality commonly found in synchronous software packages. The names of these functions and the buttons or menu choices in your course may vary from those used in this text. Two of the most popular software vendors, Centra and Interwise, require that a software program be installed on the participants' computers prior to attending live courses. If you are responsible for the installation of the course software, basic computer skills and knowledge of Microsoft Windows is recommended in order to complete the technology steps identified in this chapter. These topics are explored in detail in the previous chapter. *Note:* Some of the technology installation steps may have already been completed by your company's or school's IT department.

After completing the One Hour Before Course Start Time checklist, you should arrive in the course fifteen minutes before the course starts. In a classroom course, you would normally spend this time introducing yourself to classmates and sharing personal information about who you are and your interests. You may do the same thing in synchronous courses. This also helps with your mindset at the start of the course.

While Waiting for the Facilitator to Begin

- Clear your mind of your daily activities.
- Plan how to participate.
- Introduce yourself to classmates.
- Practice using the synchronous software capabilities.

While you are waiting for the course to begin, clear your mind of your daily activities and current work. The most effective way to focus on the course is to "chat" with other participants. Most synchronous software provides two ways to chat with others in the course. You may use the voice over IP (live audio) to speak with others or you may use a text chat feature.

Another strategy is to review your plan for participation in the course. In many ways a synchronous course is learner-centered, and the responsibility for connecting to the course and initiating communication with the facilitator and other participants is yours.

As other learners join the course, send them notes or participate in chat room discussions. It is the equivalent of getting to know your classmates at the start of a classroom course when you connect with people online. You may also greet the facilitator and ask questions about the topic. As you use the capabilities of the software to communicate, you will become comfortable and the software will tend to fade into the background, allowing you to concentrate fully on the course presentations and activities. This is identical to driving a car. The first few times behind the wheel you are so focused on the controls such as steering, acceleration, and braking that it is difficult to pay attention to other vehicles on the road. As you gain experience in driving, your focus on the controls shifts to the background and you are able to give most of your attention to what is happening on the other side of the windshield. One recommendation that was made in the previous chapter to help you quickly move to this level of comfort with the synchronous software is to attend a demonstration by the vendor of the software you will be using. These are often available on the vendor's Web site. Next, let us examine the specific capabilities of synchronous software that allow you to communicate with the facilitator and co-participants.

SYNCHRONOUS SOFTWARE CAPABILITIES

As indicated previously, at this point you may have installed synchronous software on your computer and logged in to a Web site to access the synchronous course. Once you are in the course, the window that provides the view of the course content also contains controls that allow you to interact with the facilitator and other participants, as shown in Figure 5.1.

Figure 5.1. Interwise Buttons

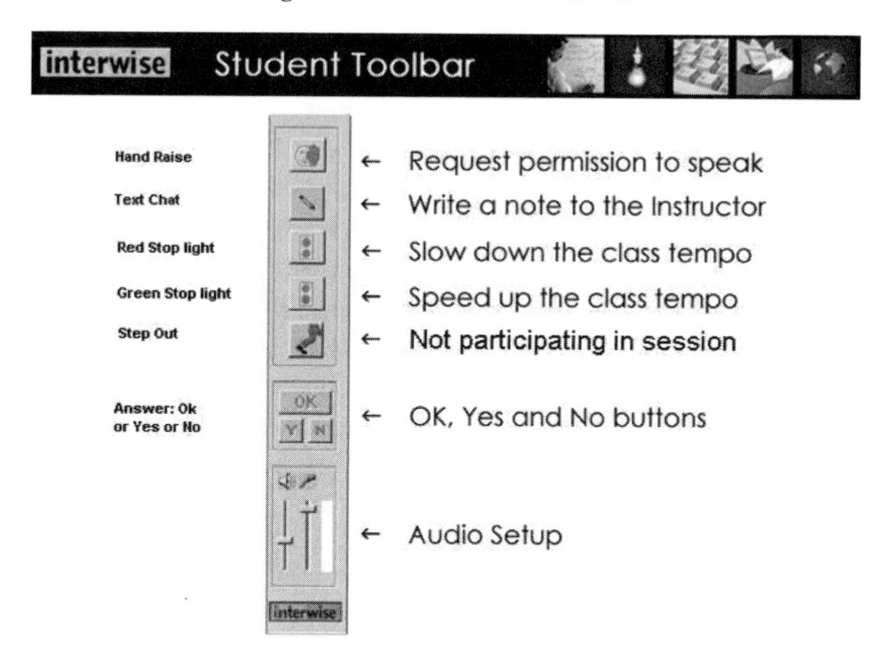

The graphic shown in the figure is a screen capture of the left edge of the Interwise participant interface. Notice that starting in the top left corner are five buttons that provide ways to communicate with the facilitator: Hand Raise, Text Chat, Red Stop light, Green Stop light, and Step Out. Below them are response buttons for OK, Y (yes), and N (no). At the bottom are the volume controls for your computer speaker and microphone. Later you will see a comparison between Interwise and Centra for each of these capabilities. Next, let's examine the function of each button in Interwise.

Function of Buttons in Interwise

The top button, which looks like a face with a hand held up, is used to signal the facilitator, both visually and with an audio tone, that you have a question or wish to speak. The second button looks like a pencil. When clicked, a message window is opened that allows you to send a text message to the facilitator. If more than one facilitator is in the course, then it will be sent to all facilitators. This allows one of the facilitators who is not actively presenting to answer your question. When answering, the facilitator may send the response back to you as a private message or to all participants in the course as a public message. The two stoplight buttons allow you to send anonymous indicators to the facilitator, requesting them to slow down or speed up the delivery of the presentation. The fifth button, the one that looks like a pair of legs, can be used to indicate that you are temporarily leaving the course, without logging out. You can use this to indicate that you are getting a drink, answering an important phone call, or in some other way not actively participating in the course. The three response buttons, OK, Y, and N, are used to answer verbal questions asked by the facilitator. The participant interface is shown in Figure 5.2.

Notice that in this image, a number of the buttons are "grayed out" for example, the OK, Y, and N buttons. This indicates that

Figure 5.2. Interwise Participant Interface

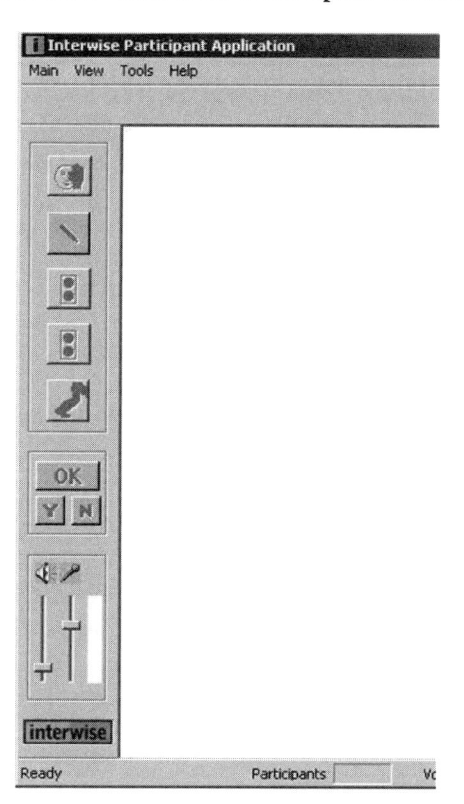

the function is not available. When the button is "live," as indicated by it being in color, you may use the capability. There are many things that control whether or not a function is available. The first is that you must be logged in to a live course. Second, some buttons are activated by the facilitator at particular times in the course. For example, if the facilitator asks a question requiring a Yes/No response, the facilitator must activate that button for you to respond. Third, buttons may be turned off by the software. For example, if the facilitator has turned on your Internet microphone, in effect giving you permission to speak, the Hand Raise button is automatically deactivated.

Audio

The use of audio over the Internet is controlled by a number of features in your computer. You can use the slider bars in the participant software to control the volume or the Microsoft Windows volume control and mute function. If the microphone or speakers are muted, they are not available for use. If you are having problems hearing or speaking in the course, refer to the audio testing portion in Chapter 4 for detailed troubleshooting information.

Video

Some synchronous software supports the use of live video images. This requires that the person have a Web camera connected to his or her computer. The video feed may be adjusted so that only a still image is displayed on your computer or a continuous image, as you see on TV. If the image is jumping or not providing smooth picture transitions, this may be caused by a low bandwidth connection to the Internet or by the facilitator setting the video rate to a low value. Normal television signals are at thirty images or frames per second. Internet Web cams may be set at slower rates, such as five, ten, or fifteen frames per second. Using these lower frame rates reduces the amount of data sent over the Internet.

WAYS TO INTERACT WITH CO-PARTICIPANTS

Next, let's examine ways you may communicate with other participants in the course. Some functions include identifying who is in the course; private text messaging; audio capability; chat rooms; whiteboard paint tools; whiteboard text tool; bulletin boards; and instant messaging.

Most synchronous software displays a list of the people logged into the course with icons that look like a little face next to each name. The shape of the icon indicates which people are facilitators or participants and the functions that each may use. See Figure 5.3 for an example.

Figure 5.3. Icons Showing Class Members

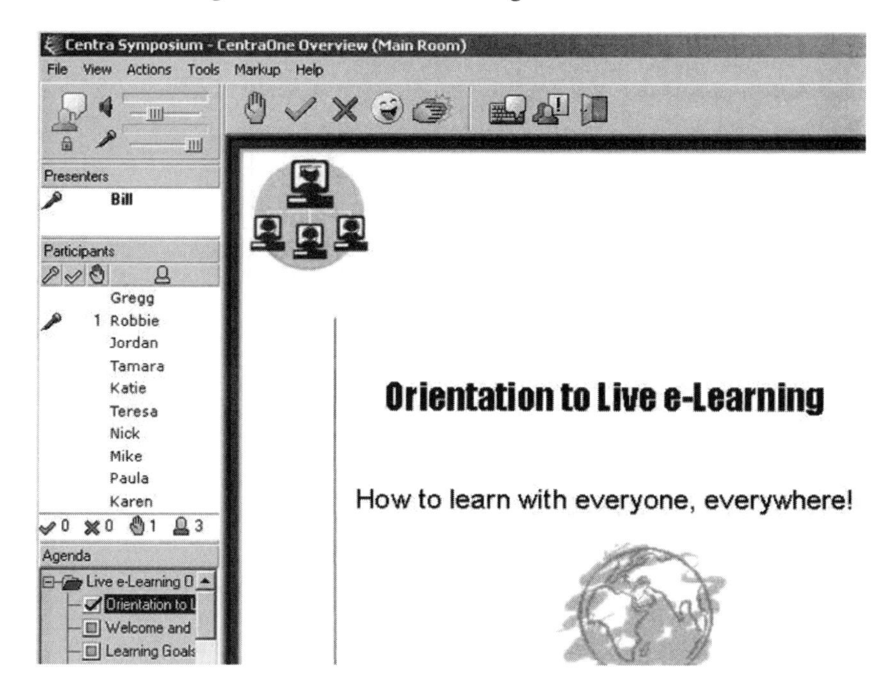

The list also provides information about the attendees and access to them through a variety of capabilities. Often, when you move your mouse pointer over one of the names, additional information is displayed about the person, such as last name or location. Figure 5.4 is a screen capture of the Centra participant interface. The buttons look different from the Interwise interface, but they perform many of the same functions.

Figure 5.4. Centra Participant Interface

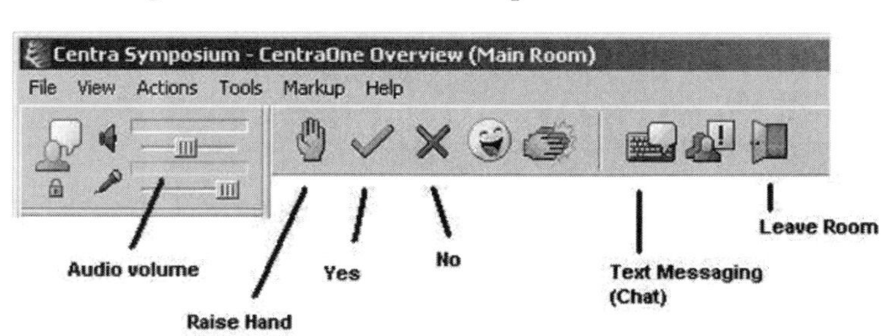

Table 5.1 provides a comparison between a few of the interaction buttons in the two software interfaces used as examples here.

Table 5.1. Comparison of Features

Feature	Interwise	Centra
Raise Hand	Face with Hand	Hand
Text Messaging	Pencil Icon	Keyboard with Bubble
Answer Yes	Y	Checkmark
Answer No	N	X
Step Out	Leg Walking	Leave Room
Speaker Volume	Slider Bar	Slider Bar
Microphone Volume	Slider Bar	Slider Bar

The shape of the icon associated with the name may also change based on your rights in the course. If you raise your hand by clicking the "Hand Raise" button in Interwise, a hand is displayed next to your "face," indicating that you have a question. In Centra a number appears next to your name. To give you speaking rights, the facilitator double clicks on your icon (or name). Most software indicates which people are speaking over the Internet by changing the color of their icons. Usually two people may have the microphone at a time, the facilitator and one participant. By monitoring the color of the icons, you can tell which person is speaking. Normally, the people who have speaking rights are also able to control the presentation pointer and the paint mark-up tools, shown in Figure 5.5.

Figure 5.5. Controls for Centra Mark-Up Tools

Using the paint drawing tools, participants can highlight portions of the screen by underlining or circling words using the yellow box or pencil in Centra. The text tool allows them to enter words on the screen that everyone sees. When participating in a brainstorming course, this is one way you may give your response. Remember: Only people who have their microphones on are able to use the mark-up tools.

If you right click on a person's icon, other options may be listed, such as the ability to send a private text message to one person. You may wish to compose the message in a word processing program first, run spell check, and then copy and paste the message to the message window.

The facilitator often has access to additional functions, such as starting a private conversation, viewing a participant's computer screen, or disconnecting a person from the course. Other ways you may be able to communicate with your fellow participants can include chat rooms, bulletin boards, or instant messaging.

In a virtual course, the facilitator has many indicators to gauge your reaction to the content and to assess your level of understanding. The tone of your voice, your response to questions, and the types of questions you ask are all indicators facilitators use to replace the monitoring of eye contact and body language. Other tools include the speed of your response to requests to click on "OK" if you are ready to proceed and the completion of online assignments. At times it may feel like the facilitator can see what you are doing as though he or she were sitting with you at your computer.

RECOMMENDATIONS

Now that you are familiar with the tools and information available, let's explore some recommendations for their use.

During the course, use the tools to interact often with the facilitator and other participants. This will help you stay focused on the content of the presentation. Develop good work habits, such as taking notes, promptly answering questions, and responding to surveys.

These offer a no-risk way to test your knowledge because they are normally not graded.

During the course, follow the guidelines established by the facilitator. These guidelines should be provided before the first course or right at its start. If the guidelines are not provided, ask the facilitator how questions will be handled:

- Should you ask them at the end of each presentation?
- At the end of a major concept or at any time during the course?
- Should you use the hand raise function to signal the facilitator when you have a question or should you send him or her a note?

Ask your questions at the appropriate time in the content sequence by listening for related content. When you receive an answer, record the answers on your sheet containing the questions you prepared before the course. Near the end of the course, review your list of questions to determine which were not answered. If the course content does not relate to some of the questions, save them for a course that does or email the question to the facilitator. Developing these effective behaviors will result in a positive experience and a positive attitude regarding synchronous courses.

WHY WORK SO HARD?

By now you are probably wondering why you should work so hard to prepare for and participate in the synchronous course.

The answer is in the value you will receive from taking these steps. Your time is valuable, your facilitator's time is valuable, and the costs associated with scheduling and delivering the course have value. These costs include the preparation of the presentations, connection costs, software license fees, and the cost of special computer equipment for servers, audio, and video. On the other side of the balance sheet is the benefit you receive from the knowledge gained and the new friends you meet online. This completes the examination of attending your first synchronous course. Next, let's explore the similarities and differences between the first course you take and subsequent courses.

In the previous chapter, "Preparing to Attend a Synchronous Course," there were many differences identified between preparing for the first course and preparing for subsequent courses. When attending a course, there are very few differences. In many ways it is like having a home office. If your home office is set up in a permanent location with all of your materials, equipment, and supplies ready to use you may sit down and begin working. If your home office is the kitchen table, then each time you sit down, you must start by setting up your computer, unpacking supplies, and arranging your work area. The same concept applies to attending a synchronous course. Just like a telecommuter, if you are connecting from a temporary space, then you must do the complete set-up for each course.

While attending the course, the only difference between the first and subsequent courses is that in the first course you learn the ground rules, how the facilitators interact with you, and their expectations. The steps to prepare your mindset, review the content, and participate in the course occur for each synchronous course.

Attending Subsequent Courses

1. Prepare your mindset.
2. Review content.
3. Plan questions.
4. Check for additional facilitator communications.
5. Set up in the location from which you will attend half an hour before the course start time.
6. Close other applications, especially any that use the Internet such as instant messaging.
7. Log on to the course fifteen minutes before start time.
8. Launch a word processor for spell checking of text messages.

SUMMARY

This completes your examination of attending a synchronous course. In this chapter you reviewed things you must do to prepare for attending a synchronous course, things to do that will increase the likelihood of having a positive and fun experience, and capabilities of the synchronous software that allow you to do many of the same activities as in a classroom course. Throughout the chapter, you explored strategies to receive the most benefit from the time you are online. Attending a synchronous course can be a very rewarding experience, allowing you to meet people from around the world, have firsthand access to experts, and take the opportunity to participate in focused discussions. To a large degree your experience while attending depends on your preparation and application of the concepts identified in this chapter.

About the Author

Bill Knapp is a senior manager in the Learning Edge Group in Deloitte Consulting and is responsible for global virtual learning infrastructure. In this role he is responsible for the deployment of internally developed distance learning courses, supporting infrastructure, and technical training of distance learning instructors. During his career, he has developed a wide range of training materials for synchronous courses, asynchronous learning content, self-study workbooks, multimedia presentations, live action videos, and classroom-based courses. At Deloitte he has developed and delivered courses globally, both in person and over the Internet, addressing the local needs of learners in countries such as Japan, China, Singapore, Holland, Germany, Italy, and the United States.

Knapp has more than twenty-five years experience as a professional educator, delivering courses in both the public and private sectors. During his career he has specialized in technology training, delivering topics such as computer-aided drafting, robotics, and ERP solutions.

Chapter 6

Succeeding in an Asynchronous Environment

Harvey Singh

ASYNCHRONOUS LEARNING is perhaps the most flexible form of learning in terms of scheduling, sequencing, and pacing your learning experience.

This purpose of this chapter is to familiarize you with the key elements of an asynchronous learning experience and to provide you with strategies for becoming an effective asynchronous learner. Through consistent use and application, you can turn these strategies into successful habits of effective asynchronous e-learning!

ASYNCHRONOUS LEARNING

The most important attribute of asynchronous learning is that you can access the e-learning content or course and participate in learning activities and interactions with other participants and facilitators at your own time and pace. In other words, you don't need to access the e-learning environment or content at the same time as others.

Typically, the asynchronous e-learning environment and content are offered via a Web server and accessed through a Web browser.

Alternatively, at times, you may also have access to asynchronous digital content distributed on a disk or CD-ROM so you can, for example, access it from a laptop without being connected to the Internet.

There are two key components of an asynchronous learning experience: the learning environment and the e-learning content.

You must understand the difference between these components and leverage them both to maximize your learning.

The Learning Environment

The learning environment or the management system provides the functionality to find, launch, and view multiple pieces of content. In addition, learning environments provide functionality that may be common to different content modules, for example, registration, security, scheduling, reporting, and so forth.

Typically, when you're given access to an asynchronous learning environment, you'll be provided with a home page, a personalized learning page that contains all the content or courses that have been assigned to you. In addition, you maintain your own preferences and profile information.

E-Learning Content or Course

The content is the most significant aspect of the asynchronous learning experience. The content can be designed to run within a learning environment or learning management system, or it may be launched and viewed independently of the environment (for example, delivered on a CD-ROM).

The most common forms of e-learning content include:

- Web-based multimedia tutorials, lessons, or courses
- Simulations (usually structured around job tasks, scenarios, procedures, products, or physical environments)
- Assessments—a series of online questions such as multiple choice, fill-in-the-blanks, drag-and-drop, and others
- Documents—cases studies, stories, procedures, and so forth

Self-paced e-learning content or courses may be supplemented by asynchronous collaborative activities such as e-mail and Web-based discussion forums. You can use these tools to communicate with your peers and facilitators.

SEVEN HABITS OF HIGHLY EFFECTIVE ASYNCHRONOUS LEARNERS

Just as with most other skills, you can practice and hone your asynchronous learning skills and turn them into habits. Here are some hints for you.

Develop a Spirit of Lifelong Learning

First and foremost, you must cultivate a spirit of lifelong learning, in contrast with the traditional attitude toward learning wherein the instructor drives the learning process and learning is confined to the boundaries of time and space, that is, the physical classroom.

Many asynchronous learning environments and courses are set up as self-service Web portals (available on an anytime and anywhere basis). You need to seek out and enroll in online learning programs or courses that are relevant to your job or other career objectives.

Build Self-Motivation

An effective asynchronous e-learner is a self-motivated and self-directed learner. While being flexible, asynchronous e-learning typically requires extra motivation, persistence, and perseverance compared with instructor-led learning.

Self-motivation and discipline are especially needed for courses or knowledge portals that do not offer a human facilitator or expert. The following will help you:

- Prior to your e-learning experience, set your learning goals and objectives and match those goals with the job requirements and business objectives.

- Discuss your goals and objectives with your manager or supervisor to set priorities and measurable milestones.
- Measure your progress against the goals and adjust the pace or content to realign the learning path with the goals.
- Learn to use the annotation or notes feature to record your thoughts, questions, and key points.

Here are some additional techniques your can use to become a more effective asynchronous e-learner:

- Log on to the learning environment regularly and check for any messages and notification and, in a facilitated asynchronous course, prepare for each class by reading ahead, completing online assignments and tests.
- Avoid procrastination and postponement of learning activities;
- Define and exceed your own milestones and targets.
- Motivate yourself by rewarding yourself for achievement of milestones.
- Find a buddy or a mentor to validate and facilitate progress; in job-related e-learning, this could be your peer, supervisor, or manager.

Hone Time-Management Skills

An effective asynchronous learner exhibits adeptness in time management. Time management is more critical in an asynchronous e-learning environment than in a traditional classroom-based instruction since the content is primarily designed for self-paced delivery. Self-discipline is the key to success.

Key time-management strategies include:

- Allow adequate breaks from work to schedule online learning activities.

- If available, use the calendar feature of the learning environment to schedule the learning activities.
- Remove any distractions from your work environment or find a quiet place to learn.
- Jot down important ideas or print cue cards or job aids (reference information that can be used on the job) for quick reference or review while away from a computer or Internet access.
- Take frequent breaks during the learning process to absorb new material.
- Pace yourself during the learning phase; if you get stuck, place a bookmark and revisit the activity or immediately send an e-mail to remind yourself or seek external guidance.
- As applicable, educate your manager or supervisor about the benefits of e-learning and negotiate the time on the job to devote on learning online.

Embrace Web and Technology

The Internet and Web are fast becoming the primary medium for interactive communication and knowledge transfer. In addition, the Internet and computer technologies are continually evolving. Effective learners remain open to new technologies and master the basics in order to benefit from new services and content delivered on this new medium.

At the basic level, you need to invest time upfront to become comfortable and confident about basic computer hardware and software setup. For example, you need to know how to connect the computer to the Internet, operate the CD-ROM drive, maneuver audio-video controls on the computer, and become adept at the use of Web browsers and other software applications to browse different Web sites and e-learning content.

Some of the other key skills include effective search skills to locate the appropriate learning resources on different Web sites or within knowledge and learning management systems.

Take some time to quickly familiarize yourself with the asynchronous learning environment and content structure before proceeding with the learning activities. Here are some of things to look for.

In the learning environment use these features:

- Notification area with assignments, due dates, and content updates
- Personal or "My Learning" page to manage learning activities and assignments
- Personal profile and calendar features (if available) within the learning management environment

Bookmark the content and the learning management environment and visit it frequently to check for updates, notification, and messages. In the content take note of the following:

- Content navigation, that is, the table of contents, toolbars, and icons corresponding with different functions such as bookmarks, annotations, calculator, and so forth
- Content structure such as hierarchical, hyperlinks, layered, pretests and post-tests

Also test your computer's audio-video connections to ensure that content with audio-video elements will play appropriately.

Build Collaborative Community

An effective learner thrives in a learning community. The learning community may mean a correspondence with a learning buddy at the same location or thousands of miles away or a very large group of individuals sharing a common purpose or learning objective.

The benefits of learning within a community include:

- The ability to widen the scope of learning by getting multiple experiences and points of view
- A chance to expand on the structured learning experience by inviting an unstructured dialogue with peers and experts
- A learning buddy or team that helps motivate, validate, and reinforce new learning
- Sharing knowledge in an online learning community (by posting comments in discussion forums, articles, "knowledge nuggets," or tutorials in a common knowledge base), which establishes your credibility as an expert and promotes your ability to seek mentorship of others when needed
- Supporting others by asking the right questions and helping others

The completion rates for learning programs have been demonstrated to jump dramatically with the inclusion of communication with experts and peers using e-mail and discussion forums.

While fostering sense of learning community, effective learners also follow the norms of "netiquette":

- Refrain from personal attacks as they draw energy away from the learning process.
- Exhibit patience, especially when dealing with asynchronous communication and collaboration since the other participants may not be available immediately after your question or request has been submitted into the system.
- Avoid casual and personal chats that are not directly related to the learning topic.
- Keep your message succinct and direct; avoid long, verbose diatribes.

- Observe any specific guidelines and rules of conduct set up by the moderators of discussion forums and chat rooms.

Apply Accelerated Learning Techniques

Asynchronous content is primarily designed for self-paced learning, that is, allowing the learners to learn at their own speed. Effective learners know how to optimize their learning time. Here are some of the strategies applied by the e-learning pros:

- Always learn with a purpose in mind, for example, start your learning by setting specific objectives of your own rather than depending passively on the expert's objectives and opinions; formulate some questions in your mind based on keys: who, what, where, when, how, why.
- Quickly scan the content before diving into the details; in particular scan the table of contents, titles and subtitles, underlined and bold text.
- Learn in phases from broad to detail levels.
- Read critically, challenging the content designer's views rather than passively accepting the content or the view presented by the course designer or subject-matter expert.
- Become an active learner, that is, adapt the content to your own interest and needs; remove the feeling of guilt that you must read and view each and every frame in order to get the most out of the learning unit; each learner has his or her own definition of completion unless bound by some regulatory agency to read and comprehend each and every frame/page of content.
- Take a pretest (if one is available) before diving into the content, as this will jog your mind and prepare it for the new concepts and will allow you to focus on the areas with greater gaps in your knowledge or understanding.

- Visualize the content by using the visuals and animation as a guide and starting point for your own visualization of the subject-matter expert's or designer's illustrations.
- Leverage the multimedia capabilities of the content to suit your learning style.
- Take extra time to engage in the practice activities and simulations exercises as learning by doing is the best possible way to maximize your learning, retention, and application of new knowledge.
- Create a mind map after viewing and practicing a learning unit or lesson; create a circle and label it with the key word or phrase representing the central idea of the content; add branches and subbranches representing related concepts, facts, procedures, and so on; annotate the content whenever possible and revisit your notes as often as necessary.
- Ask questions or provide feedback to the authors and designers about the content in order to further refine your understanding and build and leverage a network of peers and experts in your ongoing quest for learning.

Take Action

Finding opportunities to apply what has been learned is the best way not only to solidify your understanding at the conceptual or cognitive level, but also to create ownership of the knowledge and translate that learning into emotional or physical levels. Here are some action hints:

- Identify and define job-related tasks that exhibit the behavior that has been learned and apply your knowledge to perform those tasks.
- Depending on the circumstance or job-task involved, the application of knowledge may require mentoring from an expert.

- Become an action-oriented e-learner by reviewing the content as appropriate and reflecting on what has been learned and applied.
- Make notes about your new learning and the application of the new knowledge; send an e-mail with questions and comments related to your learning and share ideas with others (peers, supervisor, manager).

SUMMARY

Asynchronous learning—the ability to learn at your time, pace, and space over the Internet—is perhaps the most common and necessary component of any e-learning experience.

The combination of the e-learning environment or management system and the e-learning content or courses constitutes the asynchronous learning experience, and you need to leverage both to maximize your learning.

The blending of asynchronous self-paced (online documents, multimedia tutorials, simulations, and assessments) and asynchronous collaborative learning (through email, discussion forums, and assignments) results in superior asynchronous learning experiences.

By inculcating the seven habits of highly effective asynchronous learners described in this chapter (spirit of lifelong learning, self-motivation, time management skills, technology savvy, collaborative engagement, accelerated learning, and action-oriented follow-through), you can derive the most benefit from your asynchronous learning experience.

About the Author

Harvey Singh is the founder of NavoWave, Inc., an e-learning and e-performance solutions company. Considered a pioneer in e-learning, Singh has directed numerous e-learning programs and designed one of the first learning object and SCORM- (e-learning standards initiative) based learning content management systems. He has more than a decade of experience in the distributed learning and knowledge management fields and is noted as one of the early proponents of an integrated, standards-based approach to enterprise learning. Singh has consulted with major organizations such as Microsoft, Oracle, Sun Microsystems, Harvard Business School, and the Department of Defense on their e-learning initiatives. He has graduate degrees in computer science and education from Stanford University and a bachelor's degree in computer science from North Carolina State University.

Chapter 7

Chat Rooms and Discussion Boards

George M. Piskurich

AS AN E-LEARNER, you will sooner or later be asked to participate in chat rooms or discussion boards. These activities provide some of the person-to-person interactions that are lacking in asynchronous programs and give you both time and opportunity to explore more specific topics (and people) after attending synchronous sessions. Both of these processes are covered in later chapters in this book as part of "Understanding Online Relationships" (Chapter 10) and "Participating in Group Projects Online" (Chapter 11). However, they are so important to the e-learner that we thought we'd give you a chapter that explores them specifically.

UTILIZING CHAT ROOMS EFFECTIVELY

E-Learning chat rooms work in basically the same way as any chat room on AOL or Yahoo. You interact with other learners by typing in a message that immediately (more or less) appears on the other person's screen, and he or she responds to you in the same fashion. You may interact with only one other learner or with a group, depending on the plan set up by your facilitator. You may join a chat room to discuss a specific question or problem put forth by the facilitator, to talk about a problem or question you and other learners have with the content or assignment, or simply to discuss anything that comes to mind, preferably concerning the topics developed in your e-learning course.

Chat rooms may be limited to a certain period of time after each session, or they may be online continuously as long as the course is running. They may be monitored by a facilitator or not.

Interestingly, the depth of interaction that occurs in a chat room is often much greater than that during a synchronous session, or even in a live classroom. You have more time in a chat room to think about what your fellow learners are saying and to respond to them. Also, your instructor, if he or she is participating, has time to listen to what you and your colleagues are asking and to reflect on the best ways to move the discussion. So don't be too surprised if he or she does not immediately answer your question, but waits for more information to appear from your fellow learners.

You may also find that you are more comfortable interacting online, as you not only do not need to think as fast, but you can remain anonymous if you wish. Most e-learning chat processes allow you the choice of "signing" your comment or not.

Some learners are uncomfortable with the use of chat rooms, as they want to hear (read) what the instructor has to say and not listen to their classmates, who may know no more than they do. However, it's important to realize that you can learn from everyone, particularly in a business environment where your fellow employees from other parts of the company may have better ways to do things than either you or your instructor might have considered.

One of the disadvantages of a chat room is that it is usually set up for a specific time, particularly if a facilitator is going to be present. This means that, like in a classroom or synchronous e-learning program, you need to be there when things are happening. On the other hand, if you are a bit of a procrastinator this adds a little structure and focus to your learning, particularly if you need to prepare for the online chat.

How to Effectively Participate in a Chat Room

- Value your colleagues' opinions.
- Use emoticons, but use them sparingly (see Chapter 10 and suggested resources).

- Don't use chat time to ask personal or administrative questions, but use it to explore and interact.
- Don't be a "chat hog," but give your other colleagues a chance to respond.
- Take private or off-the-topic discussions offline using a bulletin board, or simply e-mail.
- Even if a colleague gets angry, keep your cool (it's hard to shout over a computer anyway).
- Keep your comments short and to the point.
- If you don't want to be anonymous, identify yourself at the start of your message.
- Think before reacting to a comment.
- It's hard to tell a joke in a chat situation.
- It's even harder to be sarcastic.
- There is never a good reason for an obscenity.
- Remember that everyone may not know acronyms that are very familiar to you, so spell it out.
- Keep your comments to the point, as this is no place for showing off what you know.
- It's OK to lurk for a while, but then jump in;
- Be sure to introduce yourself.
- There is often a delay in postings, so be sure you are responding to the right posting.
- Use spell check.

PARTICIPATING IN A DISCUSSION BOARD

Discussion boards are also called bulletin boards, threaded discussions, forums, and other related terms. They are termed asynchronous activities, as they do not occur at a particular time but are available when you have the time to read and react, usually continuously during and often after a course or program. This provides you with more time to think before reacting, and it's important to use it. Often a discussion board starts with a single question that people react to and then branches to threads and even sub-threads as contributors change the focus.

Some boards are moderated and some are not, although in e-learning the former is usually the case. This allows a facilitator to answer questions and shape the discussions, which some participants don't particularly like.

Whatever the process for your board, be sure to keep track of where the discussion is going, and most important, participate. These boards can be a great enhancement to your learning and are often eye-opening, but only if you do your part and join them.

Contributing to a discussion board is a lot like contributing to a chat room, so many of the following hints will look like those we gave you in the previous list, but we've repeated them here because they are important to each. It is important for you to realize that the main advantage of a discussion board, the lack of time constraint, is also a major disadvantage to you, as it is easy to put off checking in on the board. Like everything else in e-learning, you need to be self-directed and motivate yourself to do it on a continual, even scheduled basis.

How to Effectively Participate in a Discussion Board

- Even if your colleague makes you angry, keep your cool; capital letters and exclamation points are really not a substitute for yelling anyway.
- Use a subject line that allows your colleagues to know what you are commenting on.
- If you don't want to be anonymous, identify yourself at the start of your message.
- Value your colleague's opinions; read and think about what they have to say.
- Use emoticons, but use them sparingly (see Chapter 10 and the following suggested resources).

- Think before writing.
- Don't react to every message immediately, but instead give your colleagues a chance to respond first.
- Take private or off-the-topic discussions to e-mail, or begin another thread if you have that ability and the facilitator's OK.
- Keep your postings short and to the point; no one is going to read a whole page of your comments no matter how brilliant you think they are.
- Don't write anything you wouldn't want your boss to read; remember that electronic messages can easily be copied and distributed.
- Don't write anything you wouldn't want your mom to read; be "netiquette" aware.
- Label a joke as a joke, as your colleagues can't read your facial expressions.
- Remember that everyone may not know acronyms that are very familiar to you, so spell it out.
- Be careful not to forward a message without the sender's permission.
- Read other posts carefully before you react.
- Don't just post "I agree" or "I disagree"; explain why.
- React to both posts you agree with to support them and posts you disagree with to challenge them.
- More than about five lines is too long for a posting.
- Ask questions as well as responding.
- If you are going to go too far off the question retitle your reply and start another thread.
- Keep up with the board; if your comment isn't timely, don't make it.
- Work on expanding current threads, not starting new ones.
- Don't forget that on the Internet you are never completely anonymous.

- Think before you post, as this is the major advantage of a discussion board.
- Use spell check a lot, and cut and paste when needed.

SUMMARY

Chat rooms and discussion boards are an everyday aspect of life for the e-learner. They are found as introductions to training programs, as internal aspects of both e-learning and other training processes, and as an integral aspect of many university distance learning programs as once instructor-led courses are put online. Knowing what they are used for and following the hints we've given you can help you become an active successful participant in these processes.

Suggested Resources

Emoticons on Web

www.netlingo.com/smiley.cfm and www.netlingo.com/emailsh.cfm

Other Web Resources

http://illinois.online.uillinois.edu/resources/olo/student.html
http://mason.gmu.edu/~ndabbagh/wblg/wblg-products.htm
http://web.edcc.edu/gvb/netiquette.html
www.Distance-Education.com
www.EPALS.com
www.ffitz.com/radio/rules.htm
www.Ozline.com
www.searchedu.com

About the Author

George M. Piskurich, Ph.D., is an organizational learning and performance consultant specializing in e-learning interventions, performance analysis, and telecommuting. His workshops on self-directed learning, structured mentoring, and preparing learners for e-learning have been rated "outstanding" by participants from many organizations.

With more than twenty-five years of experience in learning technology, he has been a classroom instructor, training manager, instructional designer, and e-learning consultant for multinational clients and smaller organizations. He has created classroom seminars, OJT mentoring systems, and e-learning interventions.

He has been a presenter and workshop leader at more than thirty conferences and symposia and is an active member of both ISPI and ASTD. He has written books on instructional technology, self-directed learning, instructional design, and telecommuting, authored journal articles and book chapters on various topics, and is currently editing two books on e-learning. In 1986 he was ASTD's "Instructional Technologist of the Year" and he won the "Best Use of Instructional Technology in Business" award in 1992.

Chapter 8

Online Readings

Gaining the Most from What You Read

Ryan Watkins

WHILE THE TYPICAL E-LEARNING EXPERIENCE will introduce you to a variety of technologies (synchronous chat, asynchronous discussion boards, and so forth), to find success in most e-learning courses you will still want to be a proficient and effective reader. Despite the fact that the medium has changed and more of your reading will likely be done on the computer monitor, the essential role of reading in education has not diminished. In this chapter we will discuss the impact of new technologies not only on what you read, but on how you should read as well, since increasing your comprehension when reading materials is crucial to your success in any learning experience.

After high school and college, most of us primarily read for purposes other than "education" in our daily lives. We read the newspaper to keep up to date on world events, books for pleasure or self-improvement, and a variety of business documents for specific information. It's not that we don't learn from these reading experiences, but the reading is not for the same purpose as it is when taking an educational course or training program. The good news is, however, that many of the reading skills that you may have developed in other environments will provide you with a strong foundation for the reading required in e-learning. These skills, in addition to the skills you developed from years in the classroom, will provide you with a great starting place for success in the online learning environment. In this chapter we describe many of the tools and technique facilitated by the online environment that may enrich some of your reading habits to further improve your proficiency, effectiveness, and comprehension.

After all, reading will be an essential element of almost any e-learning experience. Whether it is reading a textbook that accompanies the course, reading the postings of other learners in an asynchronous discussion board, or getting the most out of an online article posted by the instructor, reading remains at the center of most e-learning experiences.

TECHNOLOGY AND ONLINE READINGS

Modern digital technologies have created a new world for the written word. No longer bound to paper alone, writers and publishers across the globe are continually expanding the horizons of the written word through the use of computers (and specifically the Internet). As an e-learner you will likely be exposed to a variety of these alternative media, often accompanied by the use of conventional media like the printed book or journal. The types of reading materials that you will have to purchase, or that will be furnished to you, will vary a great deal among e-learning courses. It is often to your advantage to find out the medium of the reading materials before the course begins. This will give you ample time to ensure that you have access to the required software for readings sent to you over the computer, that you have time to order necessary materials from either local or online vendors, and that you have access to technology resources required for the course (desktop video, desktop audio, and so forth). In addition, you should use the time before the e-learning experience to practice the reading techniques we will describe in this chapter. Many of the advantages of online technologies for reading (for example, document highlighters, unlimited space for taking notes) do take some practice before they are comfortable tools that can be used efficiently in an e-learning course.

Reading Online

One of the challenges many of us face when taking an e-learning course is that our reading habits are not always ideal for reading long documents on a computer monitor. As we scroll further down the page, we can often lose our place; as time passes our eyes lose focus on the materials, or other applications on our computer alert us to distractions, such as family or friends using instant messengers. Any of these, or other issues we encounter when reading online, can cause our work to suffer and diminish our e-learning experience. While online technologies can be a useful tool for us to expand our learning opportunities, simultaneously they also present us with many new obstacles (distractions) to getting the most out of the learning opportunities.

Given the decreasing costs of desktop computers and computer monitors, today most of will have access to a monitor that has at least 13.8 inches, corner to corner, of viewable space on the screen (a 15-inch monitor has 13.8 inches of viewable space and a 17-inch monitor has 15 inches of viewable space, measured corner to corner). Laptops, however, often have far less viewable space. The limited amount of viewable space complicates our reading of documents on the computer. By the time that you include menu options, scroll bars, and other selections to the computer screen, the viewable space for a text document can be quite small.

Most computer monitors offer a limited range of resolution settings to create a more useful working environment. Monitors most often offer three resolution settings: typically 640 x 480, 800 x 600, or 1024 x 768 pixels. A pixel is simply a picture element (dot) on a computer screen (Beekman, 2001). As with newspaper print, computer monitors create all images on the screen by using small dots (pixels) that when put together produce an image.

For practical purposes we will often want to change the resolution of our computer screen to maximize the information we can view (although the information will frequently get too small to read from a reasonable distance and we will again want to shift the screen resolution). You should change the resolution setting of your monitor several times, viewing different types of documents at different resolution options, before beginning an e-learning experience.[1] This will allow you to choose the appropriate resolution for your reading preference while taking the course.

In addition to resolution settings, most operating systems (MS Windows, Mac OS, and others) offer software options for the visually impaired. These options, while designed for the visually impaired, can be useful to a variety of online learners who have problems reading documents on the computer screen. You will likely want to preview these options prior to beginning an e-learning course.

Of course, if you continue to struggle reading documents on the computer screen, you do have the option of printing paper copies. Printed documents have several advantages, including portability. For most online courses, however, you will not want to print all of the documents and resources used in the course (often a single e-learning course may require that you read several hundred pages of written text). You should review the documents carefully to ensure that the materials contained within are too long to be read online and/or have continuing use in the course. Many short documents, like postings to an asynchronous discussion board, will not require printing.

Hypertext Markup Language (HTML) Files

E-Learning courses will regularly use a variety of file types to present information in the course. The first, and likely the most common, is the HTML file. HTML is the language of computers on the Internet. The specific tags (that is, codes telling the computer what to

---

[1]See /www.microsoft.com/windows98/usingwindows/work/articles/904Apr/resolution.asp for additional information on changing the resolution setting.

do with the information) make for interactive documents that can be viewed using any Internet browser (Netscape Navigator or Internet Explorer). As the reader, you will primarily see text and pictures just like you would in a printed book or magazine (although a more complex series of letters and symbols is actually informing the computer of what should be presented on the screen).

When viewing an HTML document on the computer screen using an Internet browser (for example, a lecture on the instructor's Web page), you are limited to relatively few options to assist you in reading. Internet browsers are without options like on-screen highlighters and note taking that you will find in other format readers like word processing programs and portable document format (PDF) readers. You can, however, enlarge the text of the document, which can greatly assist in reading. Within both Internet Explorer and Netscape Navigator, these options are available under the "View" menu. You may also print HTML documents or copy and paste the highlighted text of a document into an alternative word processing program like Corel Word Perfect or MS Word.

Portable Document Format (PDF) Files

Among the variety of online documents that are commonly used in e-learning is the portable document format (PDF) file. PDF files are merely images of text (or text and picture) files, very similar to a photocopy image. These images can be downloaded to an individual's computer and viewed using special PDF reading software (which is commonly free as "shareware").[2] The ability of the files to be viewed on computers using almost any operating system have made them extremely popular in e-learning.

---

[2]See www.adobe.com for a free download of a PDF viewer. A free tutorial on downloading software is available at http://newbieclub.com/cgi-bin/sgx/d.cgi?downloading-fast_learner.

The disadvantage to PDF files is that, since they are image files, the reader can only view the image and cannot edit *within the image*. However, you can edit *on the image;* when reading a PDF file you will often want to take advantage of the options available to you through the PDF reading software. These options include a highlighter for marking text, onscreen "sticky notes" for making comments related to the document, and magnification for examining details of the image that may be very small. Within some PDF files, you can also copy text to be inserted into a word processing or other document. However, not all PDF files have this option available to the reader, since the creator of the PDF document can select which options are available to the reader.

Word Processing Document Files

Within most modern Internet browsers there is the built-in capability to open a document created in a word processing program. The advantage to these documents is that the reader can edit the document while reading. As with the PDF files, the reader has options of highlighting information, making comments related to the text, and increasing the magnification. In addition, the reader can actually edit the file, making changes to the text and saving those changes to his or her own computer. This is extremely useful for e-learning courses where learners work in groups to complete assignments, because these documents can be shared and edited by group members. For example, in MS Word the "Track Changes" function can assist you in keeping track of which group members inserted or deleted which words within the document. Also, the "Comments" option can be used effectively to draw a group member's attention to specific issues within the documents.

Many of today's word processing programs also allow the writer to save a file into the HTML format. The software adds to the text the necessary tags (computer codes) to make the document appear in the Internet browser as it would on the printed page. This too can be useful if you are required to upload information to the Internet for the instructor or other learners to review.

Online Texts

There are a variety of electronic books (or e-books) available in today's market. Online books are primarily available either as downloads to handheld devices (such as Palm, Gemstar Ebook, Handspring, and others) or as interactive Web sites (such as www.atomicdog.com). E-Books come in a variety of file formats, with some companies choosing to use HTML or PDF files, while others choose proprietary software. Depending on the selection of books required for the e-learning experience, you may have to purchase additional software or e-book-related devices to obtain the flexibility of these technologies.

Online textbooks, which are available on the Internet, are likely the most common use of e-books within e-learning at this time. These interactive texts often have animated graphics, instructor notes, e-learner note-taking capability, review quizzes, online glossaries, and other features that you can use to improve the effectiveness of your reading. Some offer printable versions of the book, along with instructor notes and such, but most are only viewable one page at a time. If you do not have stable and relatively fast Internet connectivity, then some of these features may slow down your reading.

READING ONLINE: STEP-BY-STEP GUIDE TO IMPROVING READING SKILLS

How do these advanced technologies change the ways in which you prepare to read for a learning experience? In many ways they don't . . . rather they just add a new twist to many of the old techniques. We should still plan to spend time preparing to read before we actually start. This preparation will provide us with a foundation on which we can later relate information and develop a strong understanding of the materials.

Identifying the Purpose of Online Readings

Before starting it is often important to reflect on the purpose of the reading within the context of the e-learning experience (see Carter, Bishop, & Kravits, 2002). This reflection will provide you with a clear set of goals for the reading. For example, if the reading is "optional" and only an "additional reference," then you would most likely not take the time when reading to go through the details of each section or page. Rather, you may choose to review the article quickly, identifying major concepts and key points of interest.

It can be good practice to relate the reading to other activities in the e-learning experience (for example, is the reading to prepare me for an upcoming exam?). This will assist you in establishing goals for the reading.

Carter, Bishop, and Kravits (2002) identified four potential purposes for reading (noting that you may have more than one purpose for any reading event):

1. *Reading for understanding and comprehension:* Reading with this purpose commonly involves reading for general ideas and/or reading for specific facts or examples.
2. *Reading to evaluate critically:* Reading for critical evaluation commonly requires you to approach the materials with an open mind, searching for assumptions at the foundation of the writer's argument, asking questions, and comparing the readings with other materials.
3. *Reading for practical application:* Reading with this purpose usually goes hand in hand with some action (for example, reading while attempting new commands within a software program).
4. *Reading for pleasure:* Pleasure reading rarely requires that we take notes or review critical passages. Unfortunately, pleasure reading is often limited in an e-learning experience.

Knowing the purpose (or multiple purposes) for reading is essential to success in e-learning. You will want to pace your reading, select your reading environment, and choose your note-taking style based on your goal or purpose.

Previewing the Reading

Previewing the reading materials is a useful step in preparing for an efficient and effective reading experience. By previewing the materials you can identify key elements and words, structure your reading (for example, Chapters 1 and 3, then Chapter 2), identify the appropriate pace for your reading, and build a mental concept (or scaffolding) for what materials will be covered. Each of these will aid in the reading process and likely increase the possibility of retention.

In previewing the materials you should review the introduction, preface, and prefatory materials included with the book. These will provide you with additional information and often provide a context for the materials. In addition, authors commonly include tips for effectively gaining the most from the materials within these sections.

It is often useful to also review the references for an article or nonfiction book. The references will provide you with insights into what other writings are at the foundation of the author's arguments. Experienced readers can often predict the major concepts present in an article or book based solely on the references listed at the end.

Creating a Good Reading Environment

The environment in which you read is critical, and knowing which environment is *right* for you will be essential to your success. While some people can read effectively with the radio playing in the background, most of us cannot. And these environmental preferences often differ depending on the goal or purpose of our reading.

Knowing (and creating) the *right* atmosphere for your ideal reading environment is worth the time and extra effort it requires. For many of us, these considerations traditionally included lighting, noise, temperature, or other pressing interests (for example, basketball or figure skating events starting in thirty minutes). However, the online environment also offers a host of other considerations. The Internet presents us with a variety of distractions from reading. Therefore, you will likely want to turn off Internet communication programs like e-mail, Internet chat, or any instant messenger since these will often distract us while we are reading. Browsing (or surfing) of the World Wide Web is also a major distraction for many of us. Therefore, closing additional windows with Web browsers is often necessary to focus attention on the reading task at hand.

While these distractions may seem minimal, proficient and effective reading does require sustained attention; hence we will want to create the ideal reading environment on our computer as well as in the room in which we are reading.

Active Reading

Proficient reading is an active process. It involves you, the reader, interacting with the reading materials and gaining the most from the time spent. Many of the techniques used for increasing the comprehension and speed of reading in the past also apply to the e-learning environment as well. The effective reading skills you have developed should be transferable, even though you may apply them through a slightly different technique.

Questioning

Questions can provide you with an active technique for gaining the most while reading. By asking questions prior to and during a reading you can focus your attention on key facts and essential information. You can use questions to guide your reading as well.

After completing a preview of the materials, but before you begin to read the content, take a few minutes to note specific questions you have related to the reading. For example, what are the relationships among different characters, topics, or time periods in the reading? Maybe even note questions related to selected sections or pages. When possible, the questions should relate to the purpose of the reading within the context of the course. These questions can be used to acquire the essential information from the reading.

In addition, while reading you can use the questioning technique to maintain a focus on the materials. As you finish a section or page, identify questions that have not been answered up to this point. Some of the questions may be answered in the sections that follow, but others may not. Either way, by continuing to ask questions and interact with the reading materials you will be better able to maintain your focus. These questions (and their answers when available) will also provide you with study aids and advanced organizers for taking notes.

Taking Notes

Taking notes is an essential skill when reading in the e-learning environment. It is often not desirable, nor necessary, to print all of the materials you will be asked to read as part of an e-learning experience. Therefore, it is to your advantage to take detailed and accurate notes while reading the materials for the first (and possibly only) time. Taking notes can also save you time. Each time you have to go back into the e-learning environment to access online reading materials you are spending time that is not necessary. It is much more efficient to take notes while reading the materials and to refer back to those notes rather than the online materials when it comes time to compose written assignments or prepare for an examination.

When reading materials it is often useful to look for patterns in the text (chronological, place, cause-effect, comparison-constrast, and others). Effective writers will start with an outline that defines the structure of the reading; if you can decipher this outline from the reading you can often greatly increase your reading proficiency. Fortunately, clues related to a writer's outline (that is, pattern) can be identified from the section titles and headings of the materials. Using these as the basis for your note taking can often reduce your time and better organize your notes.

Writers commonly use the opening and closing paragraphs of a section to introduce and summarize the essential materials that will be discussed in the section. Reading these paragraphs and organizing your notes around their fundamental topics can also be beneficial.

Include in your notes memory aids that may be useful. Linking notes to ideas that may "jog your memory" later can be an effective study tool. Rhymes, acronyms, and other memory aids will often come to mind as you are reading the materials, so be sure to include them in your notes, as you may not remember them later.

Increasing Proficiency

While most of us read on a daily basis, for many of us reading is not a skill with which we have gained much proficiency since adolescence. We often find ourselves skimming the headlines of the newspaper or taking our time as we read a favorite work of fiction, but rarely reading complex materials in a proficient manner. And while few of us want to take a course on speed reading, there are some helpful techniques that may help us increase our proficiency, maintain our focus, and retain more information from our readings:

- Let the content of a section or page determine your pace. Allow your pace to be flexible, and don't always try to read at the same pace. Sections or pages that are outlines and contain well-structured information may be more amenable to a faster reading pace, while highly technical text may require additional attention, so don't set a single pace for the entire selection.
- Follow the major concepts and ideas more closely than the individual words. Using the section titles and headings to provide you with clues as to the major concepts or ideas will allow you to focus on the broad content rather than on the specific words of each sentence.
- Utilize the introductory and concluding paragraphs as guides for your reading. These should provide you with a sketch of

what is to come and major ideas for which you should keep an eye out.

- Have a dictionary available while reading. Don't let a limited vocabulary reduce your understanding of the materials. Use either a paper dictionary or an online dictionary to assist you whenever necessary. Often writers will try to impress us with their vocabulary, although the meanings of the words are often quite familiar to us.
- The SQ3R process for increasing reading proficiency can be of great assistance to most readers. According to Pauk (2001), the SQ3R technique was developed during World War II to assist military personnel in reading faster and studying better. SQ3R stands for *survey, question, read, recite, review.* By practicing these five steps while you read you can likely improve your efficiency and retain more knowledge from what you have read.

Reflecting On and Reviewing Notes

After taking notes related to a reading, but before you close the reading materials, it is worth taking the time to review your notes to compare them with the information in the materials. Take a few minutes to analyze the outline structure you used with your notes in comparison to the reading materials that you have now completed. Did the outline provide effective scaffolding for the reading's content? Were the questions you identified in your notes answered in later readings? Are there additional relationships among the topics in the reading that should be identified in the notes? Are new memory aids now apparent?

Reviewing your notes for completeness, accuracy, and usefulness before closing the reading materials will save you time and energy later. It should not be necessary to review the online reading materials again if your notes contain all of the required elements for your success.

Developing Your Skills

Since proficient and effective reading techniques are skills each of us must develop throughout our lifetimes, spending a few minutes after completing an online reading to reflect on the experience can be useful. Take a few minutes to note what tactics worked well with your reading preferences, what type of reading environment was the most useful in maintaining your energy, comfort, and focus, which note-taking techniques were most effective in preparing you for later use of the information, and so forth. Then note a few of the distractions that decreased your focus on the reading materials and some of the challenges you faced in effectively using the online reading materials.

We want to take away from each online reading opportunity specific "tips" for ensuring that our future online readings are even more efficient and profitable. Use the Online Reading Self-Assessment in Exhibit 8.1 to help you gauge your current skills.

Exhibit 8.1. Online Reading Self-Assessment

The *Online Reading Self-Assessment* is intended for individuals considering e-learning as an option for meeting their educational desires or training requirements. The assessment offers readers an array of questions they should consider before enrolling in an e-learning experience, especially those experiences that rely extensively on online reading materials.

Directions: Take a few minutes to review the following statements and indicate your response to each. Based on your experiences as a learner, complete the self-assessment honestly. Then add up the response values and relate your total response value to the information that follows.

Technology

1. Do you have access to adequate bandwidth (speed of access to Internet resources) to retrieve the files required for the learning experience? ① ② ③ ④ ⑤ ⑥ Not Likely … Most Likely

Exhibit 8.1. Online Reading Self-Assessment, Cont'd

2. Do you have the basic computer skills for navigating the Internet and the learning experience (search engines, downloading files, installing software, and so forth)?
   ① ② ③ ④ ⑤ ⑥ Not Likely … Most Likely

3. Is the software necessary for completing the learning experience available to you (for example, Adobe Acrobat, MS Office)?
   ① ② ③ ④ ⑤ ⑥ Not Likely … Most Likely

Preparation

4. Can you identify the purpose of reading the materials within the context of the e-learning course?
   ① ② ③ ④ ⑤ ⑥ Not Likely … Most Likely

5. Do have a reading environment that is conducive to your online reading preferences?
   ① ② ③ ④ ⑤ ⑥ Not Likely … Most Likely

Process

6. Can you identify questions that are useful in guiding your reading of the materials?
   ① ② ③ ④ ⑤ ⑥ Not Likely … Most Likely

7. Are you able to take descriptive notes related to the materials as you read them on the computer monitor?
   ① ② ③ ④ ⑤ ⑥ Not Likely … Most Likely

8. Do you make use of tactics for increasing your reading proficiency (flexible pacing, SQ3R, and so on)?
   ① ② ③ ④ ⑤ ⑥ Not Likely … Most Likely

Reflection

9. Do you adequately review the notes you take during reading to improve comprehension?
   ① ② ③ ④ ⑤ ⑥ Not Likely … Most Likely

10. Do you reflect on your online reading experiences to identify opportunities to improve your online reading proficiency and effectiveness?
    ① ② ③ ④ ⑤ ⑥ Not Likely … Most Likely

Exhibit 8.1. Online Reading Self-Assessment, Cont'd

Interpretation

Response values that total from 54 to 60: You will likely be able to benefit from a variety of online reading opportunities. Many of the skills required for gaining the most from online reading materials are already developed, so you should be able focus on the learning experience.

Response values that total from 48 to 52: While some aspects of an e-learning experience may be a challenge, overall you should have the skills for completing the necessary online readings. You will likely want to spend some additional time during the learning experience to gain the skills in those areas that you identified as being 4 or below.

Response values that total from 0 to 47: There are likely several areas in which you may want to gain additional experience before entering an e-learning course that relies extensively on online reading materials. Review the factors for which your response was 4 or below, and look for opportunities to expand on your experiences in those areas.

Note: The questions in the assessment are based on both my experiences as on online instructor and as a student, as well as on the materials I use in my course titled "Fundamentals of Success in Online Learning." As yet, the assessment has not been statistically validated nor scientifically tested. But taking each of the questions into account when considering e-learning as an option can be extremely useful.

SUMMARY

Reading continues to be an essential component of most learning experiences, whether they utilize the latest in online technologies or are presented in the conventional classroom. Therefore, in order to gain the most from an e-learning experience you should learn how to apply many of the tactics developed to increase your reading proficiency and effectiveness. Fortunately, many of the tactics used to increase speed and retention from text printed on paper also apply to text that appears on the computer monitor. There are, however, several techniques for adapting those tactics to the technology-based learning environment. As we pointed out in this chapter:

- Success in online learning requires proficient and effective reading skills.
- Some useful reading skills can be adapted from the conventional book environment, others will have to be developed for online reading materials.
- Software applications typically offer many useful tools and resources that can help you read more efficiently and effectively.
- Active reading skills can be your secret for success.

References and Related Readings

Beekman, G. (2001). *Computer confluence: Exploring tomorrow's technology* (4th ed.). Upper Saddle River, NJ: Prentice Hall.

Carter, C., Bishop, J., & Kravits, S. (2002). *Keys to effective learning* (3rd ed.). Upper Saddle River, NJ: Pearson/Prentice Hall.

Gilbert, S. (2001). *How to be a successful online student*. New York: McGraw-Hill.

Kaufman, R., Watkins, R., & Guerra, I. (2001). The future of distance education: Defining and sustaining useful results. *Educational Technology, 41*(3), pp. 19–26.

Kaufman, R., Watkins, R., & Leigh, D. (2001). *Useful educational results: Defining, prioritizing and achieving*. Lancaster, PA: Proactive Publishing.

Pauk, W. (2001). *How to study in college* (7th ed.). New York: Houghton Mifflin.

Watkins, R. (2000). How distance education is changing workforce development. *Quarterly Review of Distance Education, 1*(3), pp. 241–246.

Watkins, R. (in press). Determining if distance education is the right choice: Applied strategic thinking in education. *Computers in the Schools, 20*(2).

Watkins, R., & Corry, M. (in press). Virtual universities: Challenging the conventions of education. In W. Haddad & A. Draxler (Eds.), *Technologies for education: Potentials, parameters and prospects*. Paris: UNESCO.

Watkins, R., & Kaufman, R. (2002). Strategic audit for distance education. In M. Silberman (Ed.), *The 2002 team and organization development sourcebook*. Princeton, NJ: McGraw-Hill.

Watkins, R., & Kaufman, R. (in press). Strategic planning for distance education. In M. Moore (Ed.), *Handbook of American distance education*. Mahwah, NJ: Lawrence Erlbaum Associates, Inc.

Watkins, R., & Schlosser, C. (2000). Capabilities based educational equivalency units: Beginning a professional dialogue on useful models for educational equivalency. *American Journal of Distance Education, 14*(3), pp. 34–47.

About the Author

Ryan Watkins, Ph.D., is an assistant professor of educational technology leadership at George Washington University in Washington, D.C. He teaches online courses in instructional design, needs assessment, research methods, and foundations of success for the online learner. Prior to joining the faculty at George Washington University, he was a faculty member in instructional technology and distance education at Nova Southeastern University. Based on his experiences both as an online learner and instructor, he has published many articles on distance education and more than thirty articles on strategic planning, needs assessment, distance education, and performance improvement. In addition, he is co-author of *Useful Educational Results* (2001) and *Strategic Planning for Success* (2003).

In addition to his teaching, Dr. Watkins consults on projects related to preparing students for success in distance education and related topics for public and private sector organizations. If you would like more information, including links to many of his publications, please visit www.ryanwatkins.com.

Chapter 9

How to Handle E-Learning Peer Evaluation

Russ Brock

YOU ARE LIKELY FAMILIAR WITH the concept of evaluation. You have been tested, evaluated, and graded by teachers throughout your education. In your work setting, supervisors observe your performance, evaluate your behaviors and outcomes, and conduct performance reviews.

But what you may be less accustomed to is the process of being formally evaluated by your peers, especially when their assessment has a direct bearing on your grade in an e-learning course or with your compensation at work. The goal of this chapter is to give you greater understanding of the principles of peer assessment and provide you with some techniques for making better use of it, both in creating and in receiving evaluation feedback in your own classes.

Peer evaluation, when used in the context of e-learning, refers to *the process of having your peers systematically assess your learning outcomes (as specifically demonstrated by you in one or more learning activities) and comparing your performance results to the objectives and measurement criteria established for the learning experience*.

Among the more common formats for peer evaluation you will find in e-learning courses are

- Checklists—A quantitative assessment in which your rating indicates the presence, amount, frequency, or order of behaviors, characteristics, or conditions during the performance, for example:

Yes No Presenter used visual aid to support points

Yes No Presentation notes were sent to participants before session

- Rating Scales—A quantitative assessment that consists of one or more descriptive statements pertaining to an e-learner's performance, and which you rate by choosing a specific value from an accompanying scale such as in the following example:

	Never	Seldom	Sometimes	Usually	Always
Participated in team online meetings					
Contributed to work assignments					

- Narrative—A qualitative assessment in which you describe an e-learner's performance through supportive data or illustrative examples, either in response to predetermined open-ended questions or as a straightforward narrative report (often one or two screens in length). For example:

  Describe the individual's contributions that helped your team meet its assigned task.

  In what ways did the individual work with the team to overcome any conflict or problems in performing its task?

The evaluation data typically results in performance feedback, which you may send privately to the instructor or share with the person who is evaluated. Some peer evaluations ask you to submit your feedback anonymously; some evaluations identify you as the author.

The effectiveness of any peer evaluation process depends first on its relationship to the purpose of the learning experience itself.

Beyond this essential point, however, peer evaluations can serve a variety of purposes. They can

- Provide detailed information regarding how well you perform within a learning area.
- Contribute feedback and new ideas to explore for areas in which performance improvement is desirable.
- Offer insight into possible factors that may have prevented you from achieving certain outcomes in the course.
- Establish benchmarks for measuring your progress toward learning goals.
- Reveal areas in which instructors need to provide additional assistance and support.
- Encourage critical thinking and informed participation on the part of both you and the receiver of your evaluation comments.

Your role in peer evaluation is outlined in Exhibit 9.1.

Exhibit 9.1. Your Critical Role in Peer Evaluation

Your role in a peer evaluation process is crucial, regardless of whether you are the person being evaluated or the person doing the evaluating. The very success—or failure—of a peer evaluation depends on the following:

- Your commitment to participate fully and constructively in the peer evaluation
- The time you have available, or are willing to take, to prepare an evaluation
- The degree of objectivity applied by you and other group members in each evaluation
- A realistic awareness of your own strengths and limitations
- Your level of receptivity to performance feedback from peer group members
- The amount of training provided to you to overcome potential rating errors

PREPARING FOR AND CREATING EFFECTIVE PEER EVALUATIONS

Whenever you use the Internet to communicate with others, you are operating in a still-evolving medium with its own hybrid language, emerging rules, and style. If you are charged with preparing a peer evaluation for an e-learning course, however, the newer language form may be at odds with recommended ways for writing evaluative feedback.

On the one hand, the generally fast pace of Internet communications—particularly e-mail and instant messaging—has spawned an informality and set of unique writing devices aimed at accelerating our ability to interact with others. We find such things as conversational acronyms (where "by the way" becomes "btw"), emoticons (in which keyboard characters convey a range of emotions, such as expressing happiness with ":-)"), and hypertext links (allowing a reader to instantly jump to another Web area without finishing the content where the link is placed).

Indeed, the sheer reach and force of the Internet almost impels you to adopt such devices merely to keep pace with everyone else.

On the other hand, the nature of evaluative feedback demands writing that is clear, specific, and complete enough to properly convey your thoughts. Anything short of this causes confusion, anxiety, and defensiveness in the person receiving your evaluation.

Therefore, successful peer evaluation is as much a function of the preparation you put into it as it is of your verbal ability. At the heart of the evaluation is specific feedback about performance, which can only be obtained and assessed by your diligent work. If you create a peer evaluation without adequate preparation, it will lack the integrity and specific information required to benefit your peer members and will be regarded as less valuable by them. Some suggestions for preparing yourself for peer evaluations are provided in Exhibit 9.2.

Exhibit 9.2. Suggestions for Preparing Peer Evaluations

- Since preparation involves time, learn to manage your time to afford sufficient opportunities to observe your peers' performance throughout the assignment or course.
- When working with a small group or project team, introduce yourself to your group members if you haven't had much interaction with them during the program. Establish trust early and indicate your intention of offering objective, constructive feedback.
- Be certain you understand the purpose of the learning activity you are assessing.
- Gather the necessary performance-related information (by observing peer behaviors, writing samples, measurable outcomes, and so forth).
- Identify a clear relationship between the criteria used to assess a person's performance and the stated purpose. Eliminate or clarify ambiguous terms used in the criteria so that you know precisely what you will be assessing. Prepare your comments in the context of these criteria.
- Determine whether the feedback is to be given asynchronously or synchronously. When possible, prepare your thoughts and comments prior to a virtual meeting. This aids in developing accurate, concise statements and also reduces the time required to transmit your comments (simply copy, paste, and send). Submit your evaluation by the due date, since other e-learners may not be online when you are. This allows your fellow e-learners time to carefully consider your comments and develop reasoned responses.

Similarly, the care and thought you take to write your evaluation comments is rewarded by building a higher level of trust and mutual respect with other e-learners in your course. In turn, this leads to more open and honest communication about what effective performance is. Some suggestions for preparing written evaluations are given in Exhibit 9.3.

Exhibit 9.3. Suggestions for Writing Effective Peer Evaluations

- Know the person who will be receiving the peer evaluation and write with that person in mind (your instructor? a group member?).
- Develop your evaluation in a spirit of trust, mutual respect, and collaborative support.
- Be clear and concise, without being terse or unfriendly. Short sentences make reading simpler, but don't neglect to include important narrative just for the sake of brevity.
- Choose an appropriate tone for your evaluation (that is, choice of words and the style in which you use them). An inappropriate tone will often lead the receiver to dismiss your comments early in the evaluation.
- Proper rules of grammar and diction play a more significant role in peer evaluations than with the looser format of email messages (in which spelling, punctuation, and word usage appear to play a diminished role).
- Be consistent in the way terms are used in the evaluation. If, for instance, you refer to "managers," are you including front-line supervisors or team leaders in that definition?
- Avoid using humor and sarcasm in your evaluation comments. Humor is culturally influenced and does not translate easily among people with diverse backgrounds. Sarcasm has a high probability of alienating the receiver and should not be used.
- Even the free-wheeling Internet has its manners (netiquette). Peer evaluations, because of their sensitive nature, must stay within the bounds of good taste. You have an obligation to honor the policies of the course sponsor and the Web site host.
- Model the type of behavior or performance you are assessing in the other person. If you are commenting, for example, on a person's ability to use tact in relationships, then don't say something like "Your skills stink."

Using Peer Evaluation in E-Learning

The type of feedback you are asked to give in a peer evaluation may vary depending on how it is used in your program. The most common uses for peer evaluations include:

- Evaluating your group members on written products for the course (writing assignments, responses to discussion questions, technical reports, team research papers, and project reports, case study analyses, and so on)

- Assessing how your peers perform in regard to technical skills (safety standards, new Windows XP software, procedures for operating equipment) or with interpersonal skills (team building, leadership, conflict resolution)
- Providing feedback after you experience a learning activity (for example, peer critique of real time panel discussions, team presentations, or brainstorming sessions)
- Evaluating your group members' level of involvement and quality of contributions at periodic intervals or at the end of the course

The process by which you give the feedback may similarly vary. You might be expected to send your comments privately to the person you are evaluating, post them publicly on the group's Internet meeting site, or send them anonymously to the instructor. If your technology permits, you may even use audio- or videoconferencing that adds face-to-face communication and other interpersonal cues typically missing in electronic text-based formats.

How you send your evaluation comments, therefore, and to *whom* you send them greatly influences *what* you say in your evaluation. In most cases, your evaluation will contain sensitive information and may additionally be part of the overall course grade. You can help make the evaluation process more effective—no matter which type of evaluation is used—by following two important guidelines:

1. Be thoroughly familiar with the evaluation format and instructions *before* you construct your comments. What kind of feedback is required? What information should not be included?
2. Master the ability to send a message to a private e-mail address (peer or instructor) and to post a message on the

group meeting site or discussion area. This is a crucial distinction to make. (Imagine the damage caused by accidentally posting a peer evaluation with sensitive and critical comments to the entire group instead of the intended receiver.)

Overcoming Problems in Peer Evaluations

Evaluation, considered a challenge even in face-to-face interactions, becomes more formidable online. The barriers you may encounter during a peer evaluation process can be grouped into three problem areas:

1. *Challenges internal to the individual e-learner:* Dislike for giving feedback to others, anxiety or defensiveness to receiving feedback, biases that lead to inaccurate ratings, insufficient verbal skills, and so forth.
2. *Challenges stemming from the structure of the course:* Inability to consistently observe other e-learners' performance, pressures of work and personal lives, little opportunity for you and other learners to get acquainted during the course, potential for system failure (preventing use of group meeting site or other means of communicating), and so on.
3. *Challenges of the evaluation process:* Unclear goals of the learning experience, unclear evaluation criteria, lack of adequate training in regard to rating others, and other problems.

Another problem frequently arises whenever you are issued a group grade based on how other members of your group perform collaboratively as a team. Perhaps you prefer to have your effort and performance evaluated on their own merits. Or perhaps you consider yourself a hard-working member of your group and feel you "carry" the learners who seemingly contribute less to the group's performance or who may be "coasting" through the course. If this is the case, then you may regard a peer evaluation and group grade as unfair and beyond your control.

Despite such challenges, you can reduce many of the problems and much anxiety by initiating some simple action steps or suggesting them to the instructor or your entire group:

- Foster a sense of community early in the course, where you and your peers feel you have a common interest, trust, and level of support for open communication.
- Ensure that each e-learner assigned to your group project thoroughly understands the purpose and expected output of the project, the procedures and instructions to be followed, the terms and definitions used, and the specific criteria used for evaluation.
- Suggest to the instructor that e-learners select their own group members and consensually divide their workload in a way that meets both group goals and individual needs.
- Prepare a written group summary, agreed to by each team member, listing the task(s) each person committed to accomplish and the actual contributions made during the assignment.

Characteristics of Effective Peer Evaluation Feedback

The value of the feedback you give to your peers can range from useless to highly beneficial. The evaluation comments you create will tend to be more useful, and better received, if you strive to meet certain standards found in all well-constructed performance evaluations.

At the foundation of any successful peer evaluation is your ability to observe and think in terms of performance *behaviors*. In everyday situations, it is not uncommon for you to think in non-behavioral terms. Instead, you are likely to draw an *inference* from some kind of behavior and attribute it to a *trait* that is more generalized in nature. An example might help explain:

> Jan notices that Dana arrives late for their meeting (observable behavior). Despite Dana's apology (behavior), Jan regards Dana's lateness as being inconsiderate (inference) and then concludes that Dana is unreliable (trait).
>
> Asa, meanwhile, has observed Dana's arrival (behavior) and has also noticed that Dana apologized for the incident (behavior), promised to avoid being late in the future (behavior), and immediately focused on the task of the meeting (behavior).

The example points out how Jan jumps quickly from an observed behavior to a generalized trait. Asa, on the other hand, consistently operates in behavioral terms. Until you practice and get accustomed to this way of thinking, you may not realize how often you think in trait-like terms, for example: "He's creative" "She's boring" "They're uncooperative" "We're motivated" "She's aggressive" "He's immature."

The difference between an observed behavior and a generalized trait is an important distinction to make for this very important reason: It is possible for two individuals to observe the same behavior and have two totally different perceptions of the event. When this occurs in a performance evaluation, the effect is to render two different ratings for the same behavior. No wonder the person being evaluated may be anxious about the process!

As you develop your thoughts about evaluating a peer, you can improve the value of your comments by making sure each statement conforms to the following standards.

Six Standards for Writing Effective Peer Evaluations

1. *Objective:* Objectivity refers to the impartiality of a rating and exists when the element you rate is not distorted by your interpretation of performance or your own biases. When ob-

jective, an evaluation will produce the same feedback or rating value regardless of who does the rating.

2. *Differentiated:* The more you discriminate between key performance characteristics, the more clearly you can describe a person's performance. Ask yourself: "What specific behaviors or outcomes separate the exceptional performer from the average, the average from the unsatisfactory performer?"
3. *Specific:* The information offered by you is based on discreet, observable, and quantifiable data. As an example, say this: "The financial summary had seventeen calculation errors," instead of this: "The financial report was sloppy."
4. *Task-Related:* Rate the individual based on criteria directly related to the skills, knowledge, and abilities needed to perform the assignment and not over unrelated aspects of the person.
5. *Controllable:* Give feedback that is within the control of the person performing the task, avoiding performance aspects either influenced or changed by outside factors. Say this: "The demonstration omitted three key steps recommended by the guidelines," not this: "The presentation would have been better if all the course participants had videoconferencing capability."
6. *Timely:* In general, the sooner feedback follows the learning activity or experience, the more useful it is to the person receiving it. Avoid waiting to the last minute to prepare and write your evaluation. Do this: "Submitting weekly peer evaluations at the end of each week," not this: "Saving all the weekly evaluations and submitting them at the end of the course."

A primary reason for embracing these standards is to eliminate bias from the evaluation process. Bias results when you have a systematic tendency (a persistency) to evaluate something without regard for any actual differences that exist between factors being assessed. Ten common errors to avoid when rating e-learners are shown in Exhibit 9.4.

Exhibit 9.4. Ten Common Errors to Avoid When Rating Other E-Learners

When your peer evaluations show the following consistent tendencies	You may be influenced by this rating error
1. Rate a person high (or low) on several characteristics because you have a generally high (or low) impression of the individual in one characteristic, even though the actual performance does not warrant the rating	"Halo Effect"
2. Rate a person as average on characteristics in which you lack sufficient data; rate a person because it is a "safer" way to rate and will result in less conflict than an extreme rating	Central Tendency
3. Rate a person based on a prejudice (for or against) in regard to a certain characteristic (such as race, sex, age, values, religion); consistently rate a person's performance using stereotypes ("People who are . . . tend to. . . .")	Personal Bias
4. Rate a person within a limited range above the midpoint of a scale (generosity leniency) or below the midpoint (negative leniency), resulting in values higher or lower than deserved	Restriction of Range
5. Rate a person based on his or her presumed relationship with other people in the group	Guilt by Association
6. Rate a person based on incomplete or inaccurate understanding of the characteristic being evaluated or the criteria/terms used for the rating	Logical Error
7. Rate performance by comparing the person being rated to yourself rather than to the performance requirement	"In My Image" Contrast
8. Rate an individual unfavorably due to your own low tolerance for mistakes (regardless of whether the mistake has a bearing on overall performance) or by using excessively higher standards than the actual performance criteria	Perfectionist
9. Rate a person based on the overall learning environment of the course ("This course is good so your rating is good")	Climate Effect
10. Rate a person by remembering the first impression or most recent impression you have of the individual, while excluding other types of behaviors or outcomes made during the entire performance period	Primacy-Recency

You can go a long way toward creating a constructive, fair, and nonthreatening peer evaluation by considering the listing in Exhibit 9.4 as you prepare your evaluative comments. Well-constructed statements place emphasis on actual performance and take the emphasis away from issues of personality. They also expand the options available to your peers for improving performance and reaching the learning goals in the future.

Additional Considerations

- Before writing a narrative evaluation report, create a list of all the key performance behaviors you observed and apply the six quality standards mentioned earlier when writing your comments.
- Check your evaluative comments to ensure clear communication and test this by having a trusted friend or colleague try to rephrase an evaluative comment to determine whether it corresponds with what you had intended.
- If you feel your comments have been misunderstood, take the time necessary to state your point more effectively.
- If you feel obliged to provide more substantive critique, comment, or evaluation, create an attached file and send to the receiver's private e-mail address, including a list of additional resources when appropriate.
- When a narrative form of peer evaluation is used, avoid using vague, unspecific terms such as *usually*, *sometimes*, *often*, *few*, *most*, *to know*, *to understand*, *to show effort*.
- Note the difference between what *you* think a peer *should* know versus what the person is *expected* to know for satisfactory level of understanding or performance. Some examples are given in Exhibit 9.5.

Exhibit 9.5. Examples of Peer Feedback

The situation: A group is assigned a project to develop a business plan for a start-up business. The team researches the plan and prepares a PowerPoint presentation shared by e-mail with the entire class. Group members are asked to evaluate each member's contribution.

Examples of Less Effective Feedback:

- The amount of effort you put into the third section was not sufficient. (an inference, not a behavior)
- Your portion would have been better if it had more resembled the section I did on marketing. (bias—in my image)
- Your section was confusing and didn't fit the rest of the presentation. (lacks specificity)
- You were a big help throughout the entire class so I'd give you a bonus point just for that! (not task-related)
- Your participation was strong in the beginning, but I'd have to rate you lower because you weren't as much a leader during the past two weeks. (primacy-recency error)
- Well, nobody's perfect and nobody's all bad. That's kind of where we were as a team, so I'll rate you somewhere in the middle. (central tendency error)
- You don't deal well with conflict. (lacks behavioral specificity; lacks tact)

Examples of More Effective Feedback:

- Your section was documented with four reliable sources of evidence, which increased its credibility. (specificity)
- Your section was written with clear and concise language and included the new EPA regulations that affect this type of business. (task-related)
- When our group encounters a conflict, you can play a more effective role in solving the problem if you offer one or more options for the team to consider. (behavioral)
- You missed seven of our group's online meetings, but you kept current with your part of the assignment by calling each member and discussing what action you needed to take. You also e-mailed the team weekly to tell us of your progress. The result was that your section conformed to all the guidelines our team had established for the project.

IT'S YOUR TURN TO BE EVALUATED

The flip side of giving peer evaluation feedback, of course, is receiving feedback about your own performance.

A peer evaluation, in its purest sense, is a way to more clearly describe what makes you effective and what you can learn about yourself in an effort to become more effective. Although the intent is to give you information you can use constructively, evaluative feedback has the potential for doing as much harm as good. In light of this, there is a fundamental need for you to develop an *attitudinal willingness to seek* and *accept* the feedback of others. To your advantage, it is a disposition that transfers well into all collaborative learning and work situations.

The degree to which you are receptive to evaluative feedback rests on your mental ability and discipline to sift through trait-based or non-performance-based remarks—essentially, to go past the terms that may cause emotional overreactions—in order to discover the core feedback you can apply to your performance.

The credibility you assign to the evaluative comments—which, in turn, affects your receptivity—hinges on the set of assumptions you use for interpreting the data. For example, do you assume raters present their comments with a truthful intent? Do you assume raters are sufficiently able to recall key points about your performance? Do you assume raters have sufficient time to form their thoughts? Do you assume the raters and you share the same definitions for key terms?

A key task for you, then, is to find a way to understand what the combined statements mean about your performance. By doing so, you will be better able to gain full benefit from what others say as you work toward achieving your learning goals.

Suggestions for Receiving and Interpreting a Peer Evaluation

- Review the entire set of evaluation comments to obtain a broad context and balanced perspective about what group members say before delving into a particular evaluation or comment. Concentrating on content without its larger context limits your ability to interpret and understand.

- Read or listen carefully to be sure you understand what each rater has stated. Hastily moving through an evaluation increases the risk that you'll overlook key information or misunderstand the intended meaning of a statement. Avoid unwarranted inferences.
- You may tend to focus on comments that agree with your own opinions. ("Aha, they agree with me! So it must be *true*.") Understanding comes from considering the full array of comments—those that disagree as well as agree with you.
- You may instinctively perceive negative comments as personal attacks. The person who offered the comment, however, may have meant it in a purely positive or constructive way, but perhaps failed to properly phrase the statement as originally intended.
- Don't weigh one negative comment as being more significant than ten positive comments.
- A statement from one person is not necessarily shared by his or her peers in the group. It is simply one peer's point of view about how things are at one point in time.
- When audio- or videoconferencing is used in an e-learning course, use active listening techniques as peers offer their evaluative feedback. Invite group members to share additional information with phrases such as "Tell me more about . . . ," "I'd be interested in hearing how . . . ," or "Let's take a moment to explore more about. . . ."
- Maintain a questioning mind throughout your review of the evaluations. Take the time to honestly explore what you have learned from the comments. Think: "What additional questions or issues are raised by these comments?" "What can I do

to better understand the rater's point of view?" "What does it mean when two raters' comments contradict each other?"

- If your group has not had training on peer evaluations, set realistic expectations—perhaps a dozen or fewer well-articulated evaluative comments.
- In systems where peer evaluation is done anonymously, there is a strong urge to know *who* said something. But following such an urge will interfere with the intent—as well as your understanding of—the report. If you try to associate a comment with any specific person, you will likely add any of the biases you have about that suspected person.

SUMMARY

When successful, the peer evaluation process offers you a developmental opportunity to learn a new concept, demonstrate the level of learning attained, and receive performance feedback from different perspectives. Well-constructed peer evaluations, moreover, go a long way to help you build successful relationships with other e-learners (see Chapter 9). But when unsuccessful, peer evaluation can seriously undermine the educational value of your e-learning experience and decrease your motivation to stay active as a self-directed learner. It is therefore incumbent on you to take your peer evaluation role and responsibility seriously.

The theme offered in this chapter is that, through diligent effort, you can learn to be an effective participant in peer evaluation. The by-product of this effort is that competence in performance evaluation carries over into other areas of your life. Several key mastery areas have been offered here to help you launch your new role on a successful note, including:

- Gain proficiency with the technology and e-learning format you will use when participating in a peer evaluation process

- Interact with your e-learning group on a frequent basis (as opposed to "lurking") and strive to create a sense of trust among the members of your e-learning community
- Gain experience in accurately observing and describing specific behaviors
- Apply the principles of performance evaluation to eliminate bias and errors in rating
- Develop and nurture a favorable attitude toward openly giving and receiving feedback

References and Readings

Chute, A. G., Thompson, M. M., & Hancock, B. W. (1999). *The McGraw-Hill handbook of distance learning: A "how to get started guide" for trainers and human resource professionals*. New York: McGraw-Hill.

Johnson, C. M., Redmon, W. K., & Mawhinney, T. C. (2001). *Handbook of organizational performance: Behavior analysis and management*. New York: Haworth Press.

Mittleman, D. D., Briggs, R. O., & Nunamaker, J. F., Jr.(2002, March 2). *Best practices in facilitating virtual meetings: Some notes from initial experience*. http://mies.cs.depaul.edu/danny/GF.doc.

Palloff, R. M., & Pratt, K. (1999). *Building learning communities in cyberspace: Effective strategies for the online classroom*. San Francisco: Jossey-Bass.

Stiggins, R. J. (1996). *Student-centered classroom assessment* (2nd ed.). Upper Saddle River, NJ: Prentice Hall.

Wiggins, G. P. (1998). *Educative assessment: Designing assessments to inform and improve student performance*. San Francisco: Jossey-Bass.

About the Author

Russ Brock is managing partner of the Center for Innovation & Inquiry, an organization development and change management agency. With more than twenty-five years experience in organization development, Brock has worked with a variety of organizational systems design and change management projects. Much of his work is directly involved with corporate IT departments and network consulting firms. Prior to forming the center, he help positions as director of a management consulting agency at Bowling Green State University and as dean for the Center for Applied and Professional Education at another university, where he managed satellite distance learning programs. His current work includes helping organizations apply Web-based services for collaborative work groups and online training. He can be reached at ciigroup@earthlink.net.

Chapter 10

Building Successful Online Relationships

Doug Liberati

MOST LEARNING COMES FROM OUR interaction and communication with peers and instructors in class. Because of this, participating in group-based online learning offers more robust opportunities to develop skills and knowledge than does a self-paced, individual course. However, being able to create and maintain relationships over a distance, and through limited media, is a key skill for getting the most from these opportunities. Because of the structure and limitations of the Internet, participating in group-oriented online learning requires a special focus on interpersonal skills. Creating and nurturing a relationship with one or more people who are not physically in your presence requires a different mix of these skills than you use on a day-to-day basis.

As the state of e-learning progresses, more opportunities are arising for you to learn online with others. In some cases, you interact with others asynchronously, cooperating on learning and assignments and exchanging opinions via e-mail or discussion boards. In other cases, you interact with others synchronously, through teleconferences, live online "chat" sessions using instant messaging-like capabilities, or in more elaborate classes involving simultaneous voice, video, and data sharing. In either case, the key is that you are interacting with other people. While groups multiply learning opportunities, they also increase the opportunities for conflict.

In this chapter you will learn how to interact with others during your virtual learning experience. You will review the basics of interpersonal communication and look at the limitations placed on it by the Internet. Then you will see how the basics of teamwork relate to the virtual world. Finally, you will get some pointers on how to deal with conflict when it arises.

As you will see, the dynamics of human relationships and the infrastructure of the Internet complicate, but also add to, your online learning experience.

ESTABLISHING EFFECTIVE RELATIONSHIPS

To establish effect relationships online, first examine why you are involved with the class. Is it work related? If so, is it voluntary or mandatory? Are you excited, scared, or a little of both? Are you angry? Will classwork be on the company's time or on your own? It is important to understand your feelings because, as in "real life," your interactions with others online are colored by your perceptions and attitudes. Realize that this is true of everyone else participating in the course as well.

The next thing to do is to communicate. And this is the first obstacle you will encounter with online learning.

In a face-to-face relationship, most of what is communicated is not carried by words, but by nonverbal cues. Specific numbers can vary between studies, but it is usually accepted that 20 to 45 percent of the communication between two people is carried by words, with 55 to 80 percent being carried by nonverbal cues, such as body posture, eye contact, and hand gestures. As you can see, even in the best of cases, the nonverbal components of a message carry most of its weight.

Additionally, the words you use and the nonverbal cues you transmit depend a great deal on the rules that govern your different relationships. People understand, innately, that there are different sets of rules and norms to be followed in different types of relationships. You do not interact with your spouse in the same way you interact with co-workers and do not typically treat your superiors at work the way you treat your friends (no matter how much your superiors may claim they want you to).

These roles among people in a family or organization vary greatly from culture to culture across the world. Please note that *culture* here refers to national and ethnic culture and also, in some cases, business culture. In some cultures, communicating clearly can mean speaking very frankly indeed. In others, communicating clearly involves an elaborate effort to make a point in a way that is completely nonthreatening and un-embarrassing to the recipient. Within a culture, the nonverbal components of communication serve as useful shorthand, increasing the effectiveness and dimensionality of a conversation. Across cultures, however, they can be obstacles if you are not aware of them.

The Internet can magnify the issues of nonverbal communication and cultural difference in two ways, first by making it possible to meet people from just about anywhere, and second by severely limiting the ways in which you can interact with them.

When you sign up for an online course, the chances of meeting someone with a different cultural background are greater than in an equivalent classroom course at all but the largest, most cosmopolitan universities. And the chances of exhibiting a cultural difference are increased as well, because other participants are still in their environments and you are still in yours. After all, when in Rome, everyone might do as the Romans do; however, no one is actually in Rome in this case. Everyone (including you) is still in his or her far-off province. They, or you, may also be operating outside of their local time zone, joining in very late or very early. The chance that your fellow participants, or you, will stay true to your local culture is greater.

MEANS OF COMMUNICATING ONLINE

Once you are all together, you will find that your means of communication are limited. In asynchronous courses, you may work with only text messaging like e-mail. The primary synchronous e-learning software suppliers all provide voice transmission capability over the Internet. In this case you will also have voice inflection to work with, if not visual body language. Based on the discussion so far, you can see that these situations might cause problems, since the technology has just limited virtually all participants to only the verbal component of communication, a component that can vary widely across regions and cultures, as you just saw. No body posture, no eye contact, no facial expressions, no hand gestures, and in the case of text messages, not even any voice inflection. But just because these components do not reach you does not mean that you set them aside. You must be very sensitive to the fact that you, and most other people, have a strong tendency to insert a default set of values for the nonverbal components when they are not supplied. These defaults are usually based on the culture in which you were raised. You will read these components into the message whether they were intended or not.

As an illustration, imagine you are in an online chat session with a fellow learner. You describe an experience in which you, through inexperience, applied one of the management rules discussed in class outside of its proper context. The result was a very upset direct report and some quick damage control on your part. After keying in this message you receive the following response: "That will teach you."

Now what, exactly, does that mean? Is your fellow learner being literal, saying that this experience should help reinforce the lesson? Is he or she being cynical, indicating that he or she always knew this stuff would never work? Is he or she seeking to ease your discomfort with a little humor? The set of interpretations you insert depends heavily on your background, day-to-day experience, and mood and attitude at the moment.

In the "real world" the situation might play out as follows: You describe the situation and your fellow participant responds by getting a look of mock horror on his face, covering his open mouth with a hand and then dropping his hand to pat yours while smiling, nodding knowingly, and saying, "That will teach you." Here, the interpretation is much clearer. He seeks to share your discomfort and lend a sympathetic ear. We will see in a moment how to simulate the emotional response components of such communications in your text messages, to help assure that you are understood.

Let us recap what we have learned:

- Our communications with others are made up of both verbal components (what is said) and nonverbal components (how it is said).
- The rules we apply to our communications vary based on who we are communicating with, our respective roles, position in society or business, and perceived power.
- These rules and the definitions of roles vary across cultures.
- Most important, what is said often means less than how it is said.

Given these factors, you end up with a complex mix that assures that even two well-meaning individuals have a very good chance of misunderstanding each other, even if they speak carefully, perceive accurately, and are completely familiar with each other's backgrounds. So how can you hope to accommodate this complex process in the constrained environment of the typical online course?

Rules for Interacting Successfully Online

Because of technologically limited communications capabilities and the mix of cultures involved in its development and day-to-day use, Internet users have created their own rules of interaction as a basis for their own virtual culture. These rules of Internet etiquette, or netiquette, can serve as your guide to getting along with others online. The chart in Exhibit 10.1, Five Tips for Interacting Successfully Online, paraphrases some of these rules. Keep it handy on your first few forays into the group e-learning world.

Exhibit 10.1 Five Tips for Interacting Successfully Online

1. Remember, you are dealing with a person.	E-mail, chat rooms, and speaker phones can hide this important fact.
2. Behave in the virtual world as you would in the real world.	In a class strictly for personal development, you may develop informal friendships, complete with gossip and note passing. If you are in the course for your job, or others are, expect to develop more professional, businesslike relationships.
3. Share.	Give back to the class. Give *your* experiences, *your* learning, and *your* opinions (when relevant). You do have value to add.
4. Forgive.	Assume others in your class mean the best and that slip-ups and misinterpretations of your brilliance are accidental.
5. Communicate.	Write and speak clearly and concisely. Say what you mean and then stop. Those who are not primary speakers of the language in which the class is held will appreciate it.

One more tip: Respect people's time and bandwidth. Be sure that what you are posting to a discussion board or sending out as an email is worth the time to review by others. Additionally, do not repost items unless it is requested, post the same information to multiple areas, or post large files if you are not sure of others' Internet connection speeds. Typically, you should ask before posting files that will take more than a few minutes to download, as some users may have slow connections and will need to set aside time for the task.

For more information on netiquette, point your Web browser at www.albion.com/netiquette/. This site also contains a full online edition of the book *Netiquette* by Virginia Shea.

Internet users have also developed a set of symbols and acronyms to add nonverbal cues to their text-only messages. These acronyms and the symbols, or "emoticons," seek to provide some body language over the bodiless medium of the network.

Emoticons

If you have used e-mail, you have probably encountered the colon and parenthesis smiley face :) or acronyms such as LOL (Laughing Out Loud) or IMHO (In My Humble Opinion). In our earlier example, simply adding the smiley face emoticon at the end of the response "That will teach you" would have gone a long way toward clarifying its intended meaning. The following list includes some common emoticons and acronyms.

Common Emoticons and Acronyms

- Unhappiness = colon + right parenthesis = :(
- Undecided = colon + hyphen + forward stroke = :-/
- Surprise = colon + capital O = :O
- AAMOF = As A Matter Of Fact
- FYI = For Your Information
- HTH = Hope This Helps
- MHOTY = My Hat's Off To You

You can find a list of more emoticons and acronyms at www.pb.org/emoticon.html or at a number of other Web sites your search engine can reveal. Use emoticons and acronyms as necessary, but do not overdo it. Again, be sensitive to your group's own micro-culture and norms as they develop during the course.

Interacting in Different Ways

Here are some additional tips to use, based on the different types of interactions you may encounter in your online course.

When Contributing to a Course Message Board

- Review prework or assignments to prepare yourself.
- Review topics posted by others and contribute your thoughts.

- Remember to share; chances are you are very interested in what others think and they are interested in what you think as well.
- Be an active participant, even if you just agree or say that you echo another's experience. In a classroom people get a good idea of your stance on a subject through your body language or verbal responses. There is neither of these on a message board.

When Using Live Chat

You could also participate in a live chat or phone call as part of your coursework. Think of a chat session as an online open discussion carried out by the exchange of brief written messages, instant messaging style. Typically you log in and see the name or user ID of whoever is "speaking." At that point, you key in a response and send it, as do others. The result is a live, ongoing conversation among multiple parties. Like a real conversation, it is ephemeral in that it is gone when it scrolls off the top of the screen. A telephone conference call is similar, except that you have the advantage of hearing the inflection of the speaker's voice. The rules here are simple:

- Be prepared.
- Think before you talk (or type).
- Get involved.

When Working with a Virtual Team

You might also work as part of a virtual team. This could take the form of putting a project together through an exchange of e-mails, arranging your own phone calls outside of class time, or meeting in a virtual collaboration environment online. In this case, work with fellow team members to quickly establish the team's structure, purpose, and communications channels. If working from disparate time zones, you will need to find a way to work asynchronously.

Additionally, all of the normal rules of teamwork apply as well. Since virtual teams offer the greatest opportunities and pitfalls, we will now take a closer look at them.

e-LEARNING TEAMS

If you are in a position in which you will be interacting with one or more other class members on a project, for example, to complete an assignment, then you have just joined a virtual team. All the rules of normal team formation and cohesion apply, and so do all the constraints of online communication. This is the online learning situation in which you will most likely encounter difficulty.

If you do participate in a course that requires virtual teamwork, keep the points in the Exhibit 10.2, Establishing a Successful Virtual Team, in mind as you set up your team.

Exhibit 10.2. Establishing a Successful Virtual Team

Set expectations up-front.	Arrange an initial meeting, via phone or network, where you define: • The team's purpose and deliverables. • Members' strengths, weaknesses, and level of commitment. Not everyone is good at everything. Not everyone has the same time and resources to give the project. Identify individual skills and commitment up-front.
Establish team norms.	Among the standards you may wish to consider are • What is said and done in the team stays in the team. • Share things outside the team only when the team members involved agree, or perhaps with the instructor should difficulties arise. • Create solutions, not problems. • Keep criticism on a positive note and then suggest an alternative. • Help one another.
Organize the work.	Determine what work needs to be done to achieve the purpose and deliverable within the available time. Assign team members to tasks based on the work, the course requirements, if any, and each member's talents and commitment.

Exhibit 10.2. Establishing a Successful Virtual Team, Cont'd

Track progress.	How often, to what degree of detail, and where will you track status? Did the course provider supply a tool? Define your process to keep calls or other collaborations on track.
Live up to your commitments.	Do what you say you will, on the schedule that is laid out. If you cannot, communicate this clearly and quickly to the team. Be prepared with an alternative approach.

WHAT TO DO WHEN CONFLICT OCCURS

Now that you have reviewed the ways you might be interacting online, some of the things that stand in the way of a good online relationship, and some of the strategies to overcome these factors, it is time to admit what is probably obvious to you by now . . . conflict is going to occur.

Conflict is an inevitable part of human relations. Most conflict comes, in fact, from those with whom you have the closest relationships. Think about it. How often do you argue with a total stranger? If you do, it is because you have some common goal about which you disagree. Given this, if you are part of an online relationship that is not undergoing some conflict, then it is probably not a very good relationship. It is accepted that conflict is a normal part of team development. It is not conflict that is bad, just the misapplication of strategies for addressing it.

It is important to be aware of cultural differences in dealing with conflict. Again, in some cultures conflict is expected as inevitable and unfortunate, in others it is sought out, and in some open conflict is avoided at all costs and any messages conveying conflict are carefully coded so as to avoid causing embarrassment or discomfort. So just because everyone agrees with you or any other opinion leader does not mean things are going well. Indeed, excessive agreement can signal that things most probably are not going well. Take personal responsibility for carefully listening for the signs of conflict, including silence, and become aware of the different ways you can resolve it. There are many approaches to teamwork and the resolution of conflict in teams. We will briefly examine one next.

Thomas-Kilmann Conflict Resolution Methods

In their work, Kenneth W. Thomas and Ralph H. Kilmann (1974) created a popular model of conflict, known as the Thomas-Kilmann Conflict Model. This model identifies, among other things, five approaches to dealing with conflict. These are outlined in Exhibit 10.3. Learn to spot these approaches in yourself and others as a way of resolving conflicts in your online team.

Exhibit 10.3. The Thomas-Kilmann Conflict Model

Power	You can do something, so you do it, with no regard for the rest of the group. This risks alienating people and should be used with care, perhaps only in situations in which the action being taken does not warrant consensus or the consequences of not taking the action are dire.
Accommodation	You sacrifice the goal to maintain the relationship. For example, you may yield on a particular way of approaching the preparation of your group's report to avoid upsetting your team leader, even though you firmly believe you have the better approach.
Avoidance	You walk away from the goal or task. This may happen a lot in cases of minor importance to particular team members. For example, you may not feel the need to become involved in the decision-making process about the color scheme and cover design of your group's report. Instead, you defer to the passions and talents of others.
Compromise	Each party involved in the conflict gets part of what he or she wants and loses part of what he or she wants. This is typically perceived as a good resolution to conflict, but may not be. What if there was one very good solution and one very bad one? Now you have a solution that is, at best, half as good as it could be.

Figure 10.3. The Thomas-Kilmann Conflict Model, Cont'd

Cooperation	The ideal approach to resolving conflict. Clearly express your point of view, your goal, and your needs, not just your position. Maximize your understanding of the other person and his or her needs. Reach beyond the other person's position. Be concerned with the other person's goal, your goal, and the integrity of the relationship. This approach takes longer, but results in a win-win solution that enables all involved parties to obtain what they need.

As an example of their approaches in action, think of some of the meetings you have attended, either real or virtual. Often, an issue that requires resolution will result in two sides with equally entrenched positions and no apparent way to reach a solution. You see a demand for compromise from both sides, but a lack of concessions from either. While an agreement is usually reached, it typically is not as effective as it could be, but each side feels better because it got "something" that it wanted. Alternately, Side A sometimes simply forces its way through the opposition of Side B, forcing them to do it the Side A way. This may work in the short term, but leaves bad feelings in the way of future cooperation.

The next time you are in such a situation, try to reach beyond the other person's position to get at her real needs. Often, needs and position are not the same thing. Use statements and questions such as "Help me understand this situation better" and "Let's take a look at how this approach helps us meet our needs and reach our goals." Reach beyond compromise for cooperation and remember that cooperation requires trust. As you will find, each approach in the model is appropriate in some circumstances and none is appropriate in all circumstances. Identify how you typically seek to resolve conflict and then make an effort to apply the five approaches appropriately. If your online course or courses are going to involve a lot of work with teams, you will want to read more on approaches to teamwork. A search of the business books section of a popular online bookseller revealed more than fifty titles associated with teamwork. You can doubtless find one or more books online or at your local bookstore or library that meet your specific needs.

SUMMARY

In this chapter we have focused on the issues and strategies involved with interacting with others online. You have seen that most learning comes from our interaction with others. While e-learning offers the potential for bringing you into contact with people who have a broad range of talent and experience from which you can benefit, it also limits the channels through which you can interact with them. The theme of this chapter has been that you can overcome these narrowed and sometimes nonexistent channels by understanding the fundamentals of interpersonal communication and some strategies for overcoming the technical limitations you may encounter. Specifically, you have seen that:

- Commonly available technologies do not accommodate the nonverbal components of a message well.
- Loss of the nonverbal component of communication is magnified by the mix of cultures and roles you will encounter online.
- Using netiquette can smooth communication and defuse conflict before it arises.
- Message boards, virtual teams, and live chat sessions or teleconferences each require a particular type of preparation and behavior in order to be of maximum benefit.
- Virtual teams require the same behavior as "real" teams, with the added complication of not being face to face, so be proactive in planning and activities to ensure successful team performance.
- Conflict will occur, particularly if your team is developing a strong relationship, so being aware of your own and others' approaches to resolving conflict enables you to reach the best solutions.

Developing online relationships is perhaps one of the most rewarding aspects of e-learning. You can meet, work with, and get to know people from across the country and around the globe. Handled well, such relationships can contribute greatly not only to your learning, but to your professional development and personal fulfillment.

Suggested Readings and Resources

Thomas, K., & Kilmann, R. (1974). *Thomas-Kilmann Conflict Mode Instrument*. Palo Alto, CA: Consulting Psychologists Press.

Shea, V. (1994). *Netiquette*. San Rafael, CA: Albion Books. Also available online at www.albion.com/netiquette/.

www.pb.org/emoticon.html.

About the Author

Doug Liberati is an instructional designer for LearningEdge, the internal learning organization of Deloitte Consulting. LearningEdge supports the learning needs of Deloitte's approximately twelve thousand global practitioners. The group has won numerous awards for its programs, including a 2002 Corporate University Xchange Award for aligning learning with business strategy.

Liberati has served as lead designer on several e-learning projects for the firm, as well as serving on the design and development teams for a successful series of classroom-based workshops and a set of career milestone programs that used blended learning.

In a previous position, he was an instructional designer and developer for Deloitte Consulting's client-facing learning practice, where he worked with project teams to create and deliver training for enterprise software implementations at several clients.

Chapter 11

Participating in Group Projects Online

Carole Richardson

IN THIS CHAPTER WE DESCRIBE the challenges of online group work and prescribe an approach that can help you successfully meet those challenges. Instructors use group projects because they recognize that group work encourages the learner-to-learner interaction that is essential for community building, and they know that in the workplace people are often required to function in self-directed work teams.

The complexities of today's technologically supported, information-based global workplace present challenges to collaboration in business, industry, and government. It is not unusual for deals to be made or lost based on a person's ability to work across cultural and geographic boundaries. It is not always feasible for such deal-making to be conducted in a face-to-face setting. Travel budgets have been severely curtailed for many reasons, among them a declining global economy and a desire for personal safety. Technological tools are increasingly relied on to support the work of widely dispersed business partners. To prepare learners for the world of work, it is essential that our educational microcosms not only analyze the challenges to group collaboration, but also provide experiential environments in which the skills to overcome those challenges can be groomed. Online group projects are very effective tools to help learners become comfortable working with people they never see.

The goal of this chapter is to provide you with some techniques that will help you successfully collaborate with fellow learners in the virtual environment.

GETTING TO KNOW GROUP MEMBERS

One of the most important steps to being a successful online group member is to get to know the other group members as soon as possible. Once your instructor has made it clear that group work will be required, and once your group assignment has been made, waste no time communicating with your group. Even though at this point you may not have a clear idea of the details of the project you will eventually be working on, you need to establish a relationship with the people in your group well before you begin to work toward a common goal.

Why is this? When communicating online, the absence of verbal inflection and body language to help you understand a person's meaning can create a minefield of misunderstandings and misinterpretations. The sooner you become comfortable with an individual's online communication style the better. For example, a person may consistently post one-word or two-word responses to questions posed online. "What's the weather like where you are?" results in the answer, "Fine." Reading this posted to the discussion board, members of the group may think she is rude for not being more conversational, or perhaps she is hypersensitive and offended by the question itself. After a few online discussions with group members, this person happens to mention that her typing skills are really poor. Group members who thought this person would be an annoying addition to the team now realize they jumped to the wrong conclusion. Such discoveries take time and are best made outside of and prior to the actual project work.

Use all the tools at your disposal to communicate with your team members: discussion board, chat, and e-mail. Chats are notoriously difficult to schedule because they rely on everyone being online at the same time. Even when all your group members are in the same time zone, busy lives and conflicting responsibilities complicate scheduling. The most effective tools are the ones that support asynchronous (time- and place-independent) interaction. I recommend you rely on e-mail and whatever discussion board tool is provided to you as part of your e-learning assignment.

As you practice using these communication tools, start informal conversations with your group members so that you can get to know them. When I teach an online course, I do something that I know many instructors like to do: kick things off with an *introduction* forum on the discussion board. I jump-start the conversation by asking a few f-and-f (friendly and frivolous) questions such as:

- "What was the last movie you saw?"
- "What did you like or not like about it?"
- "What is your favorite TV show?"
- "What are your favorite two leisure time activities?"

This is an opportunity to explore the interests, strengths, and skills of your fellow group members in a nonthreatening interchange. If your instructor fails to create such a forum, start one yourself. Your group members will love you for it.

UNDERSTANDING THE ASSIGNMENT

Once your instructor has assigned a project, it is imperative that everyone in your team understand the project goals in the same way. You best achieve that understanding by using the discussion board to post your interpretation of what must be done. If you take the lead in posting that description, amazingly enough you'll see many responses of "I agree" and "That's what I think too" follow. For those who indicate a differing opinion of the ultimate desired outcome of the project, it can be very fruitful to have a more immediate, real-time discussion by setting up a chat time or even a telephone call. After chatting, if there are still disagreements as to the nature of the assignment, a member of your group will need to contact the instructor for clarification. There is no point in proceeding until this agreement among all group members is reached.

DEFINING THE COMPONENTS OF THE PROJECT

As a group, you need to agree on how best to break the project into manageable parts. If every member of the team attempts to work on the entire project, you are most definitely doomed to failure. For example, for one of my online courses, I require that my learners create a budget for a major public-sector technology implementation. Each group must first "set the stage" by determining the nature and function of their fictitious agency. Then they must decide which needs exist that can be met via technology, choose what that technology solution will be, estimate all costs related to the project over a five-year time period, enter the data into a spreadsheet with appropriate formulas and illustrative charts, and provide a narrative justifying the choices that they made. It's a multifaceted and complex project and one that initially causes the learners much stress. The project planning goes much more smoothly when the group members have taken the time to get to know each other *before* they start to analyze the demands of the project.

When you work with online group projects, the last thing you need is a misunderstanding caused through an inadvertent communication faux pas. As mentioned before, you need to get to know the online communication style of each individual group member. Something as seemingly innocent as typing in all caps can set off a flame war from which recovery is difficult. You don't need that when you're working on a deadline.

DEFINING ROLES AND RESPONSIBILITIES

Once your group has segmented the project into manageable "chunks," you can come to an agreement on the roles and responsibilities of the various individuals in the group. Although this sounds complicated, it is often amazingly easy. You know your group members by now; you know whether anyone is an expert at using a computerized spreadsheet; you know whether anyone has experience with a technology implementation project; you may even know who loves crunching numbers. Group members will quite often start to enthusiastically volunteer. It's not unusual to see postings like "My best friend runs the IT department, I'll talk to her about how she puts together a budget" or "I've been using Excel for years; if someone gives me the numbers, I'll plug them in" or "I'll do a Web search and see if I can find a public agency that has that kind of information online." By now, everyone is eager to demonstrate that he or she can contribute to the project. Some sample responsibility-segments might include (using my project example):

- Gathering information about typical categories of expenditures.
- Writing the narrative: describing the agency, its function, and why it needs the technology; explaining the budget categories and the rationale behind estimated costs.
- Setting up the spreadsheet with appropriate column and row labels.
- Enhancing the appearance of the spreadsheet through the use of color, borders, shading, and so forth.
- Inputting the costs and the formulas.
- Creating the charts.
- Developing a timeline for completing the project.
- Reviewing and editing the completed project.
- Serving as instructor liaison or project manager.

Obviously, depending on the size of the group, these roles and responsibilities can be merged and combined in whatever configuration best suits the interests and skills of the individual group members.

THE ROLE OF THE PROJECT MANAGER

Don't let the word *manager* throw you off. In no way is this person "in charge" in the typical hierarchical sense of the word. Instead, this is the individual you've selected to monitor the group's progress on the project, offer reminders when deadlines are missed, function as unofficial cheerleader, and serve as group liaison with the instructor. Usually, the project manager is also responsible for at least one of the individual project components as well. It is amazing how often the group unanimously and almost spontaneously comes to an agreement on who will best serve as project manager.

Each group functions differently depending on the dynamics that have resulted from the individual personalities of group members. Still, my experience has been that the selection of the project manager is not a difficult one or one that leads to tension in the group. If there are conflicts resulting from the selection process, by all means involve your instructor. You cannot forego the option of having a project manager. The role is essential no matter what you decide to call it, because monitoring the group's progress and ensuring adherence to agreed on deadlines is crucial to your group's success.

ASSESSING THE GROUP EXPERIENCE

Out in the *real* world, there is much debate about what skills are important for a leader guiding virtual teams. Some challenges include coordinating the efforts of team members from diverse cultural backgrounds and overcoming the many logistical impediments to collaboration on a global scale. Kayworth and Leider (2002) found that effective leaders display great behavioral complexity, because they are "able to act in multiple roles simultaneously, combining relational considerations with task-oriented ones." Successful participation in group projects online requires the exercise of *people* skills at least as much as it requires knowledge and skill in the use of the technology.

When you assess your experience as an online group participant, consider the leadership skills required of each and every member of the group. Think about the elements of the experience that you found enjoyable, and develop a strategy for avoiding the ones that were not as pleasant. This meta-analysis of your online group experience should be continuous while you are in the midst of your project. Once the project is complete, you should find that you are well prepared to tackle a similar activity in the future, whether it is learning-centered or work-focused.

Use the chart in Exhibit 11.1 to help you summarize the steps to being successful as an online group project participant.

Exhibit 11.1. Recipe for Success of an Online Group Project

1. Have informal communication with your group members well before the beginning of the project.
2. Focus on building an atmosphere of trust within your group.
3. Make sure every member of the group agrees on the goals of the project.
4. Work with your group to break the project down into its component parts.
5. Work with your group to distribute the parts based on skill and interest, and develop a timeline for completion.
6. Offer suggestions for a project manager or volunteer yourself.
7. Throughout the project, live up to your commitments.
8. Assess your experience.

CONCLUSION

In 1993, distance education researcher Otto Peters stated, "As predicted for the working process, the emergence of *autonomous groups* will become the main constituent of the learning process" (p. 51). He went on to emphasize that such groups will be social environments that are supportive and "encourage spontaneity and self-expression." If you follow the recommendations presented here, it is likely that your experience will demonstrate the truth of Peters' prediction. Remember that participating in group projects in the online environment is at least as complex an undertaking as being involved in any face-to-face work team activities. The good news is that, with careful attention to clarity of communication, online group projects don't have to be any *more* difficult than any other team project you encounter in life.

Recommended Reading and Resources

Kayworth, T. R., & Leider, D. E. (Winter 2002). Leadership effectiveness in global virtual teams. *Journal of Management Information Systems*, *18*(3), pp. 7–40.

Moore, M. G., & Kearsley, G. (1996). *Distance education: A systems view*. Belmont, CA: Wadsworth.

Peters, O. (1993). Distance education in a postindustrial society. In D. Keegan (Ed.), *Theoretical principles of distance education* (pp. 39–58). Padstow, Cornwall, Great Britain: TJ Press.

Phillips, G. M., Santoro, G. M., & Kuehn, S. A. (1989). The use of computer mediated communication in training learners in group problem-solving and decision-making techniques. In M. G. Moore (Ed.), *Readings in distance education* (Vol. 2). University Park, PA: ACSDE.

About the Author

Dr. Carole Richardson holds a doctorate in public administration from Western Michigan University. She has held management positions in various organizations for more than fifteen years and has taught in public administration and political science disciplines at a variety of institutions, including Central Michigan University, Marist College, and the Saginaw Chippewa Tribal College. She is currently an e-learning consultant and an assistant professor at American University. For more detail, please visit her Web site at http://home.earthlink.net/~inali52/.

Chapter 12

Managing Distractions for E-Learners

Wayne Turmel

WELL, YOU WENT AND DID IT! You've decided to become an e-learner and use your organization's managed system that makes learning so easy to access that people can get the training they need without leaving their desks. "Click" and there it is. You'd think nothing could stand in the way now.

You'd think wrong.

Even though e-learning is more than bringing the horse to the water—frequently we're bringing the water to the horse—we still can't always make that critter drink. Why don't learners get the most from their experience? What stands in the way of a successful e-learning program? The goals of this chapter are to identify the distractions a learner encounters, discover why e-learning isn't as successful as you'd like, and find ways to overcome the barriers.

There are all kinds of reasons learning doesn't work. Many of them are unavoidable—but all too common. Learning specialists and psychologists are pretty much unanimous in agreeing that among the leading reasons learning doesn't occur are

- Poor design
- Lack of relevance to the workplace
- Learner disinterest in the topic
- Lack of rigor in monitoring learning

There's one other factor that is frequently overlooked. It is not a large line item in anyone's budget, and many training practitioners don't even think it falls under their control: the many distractions the learner faces.

Level one evaluations (the course evaluations issued upon completion of a program) from Web-based programs frequently capture statements from participants similar to these:

- "I had to answer my e-mail." (This indicates that other work pressures, real or imagined, take precedence over the e-learning event itself.)
- "There were too many distractions."
- "I couldn't concentrate for very long."

Training professionals who have followed up on those responses frequently discover that the environment many people work in every day is not conducive to the kind of concentration required for real learning to take place. This is particularly true in asynchronous learning, where you may be interfacing only with a machine without the benefit of a live facilitator or even contact through e-mail.

These distractions tend to fall into two categories: (1) *external* distractions (what's going on around the learner that interferes with the learning, such as noise, interference from co-workers and other work priorities) and (2) *internal* distractions (what's going on inside the learner's head, driven by the learner's own priorities and attitude).

In each of these there are subgroups of distractions. We'll call them (1) *environmental* (physical things like cluttered workplaces or the person from the next cubicle breathing down your neck asking, "Whatcha doing?") and (2) *systemic* (for example, management expectations that a normal workload be accomplished even during the training).

Basically, with any distraction you have three options:

1. Eliminate the distraction entirely.
2. Mitigate or lessen its effects so it's more manageable. Or
3. Work through the distraction.

In this chapter, we'll take a brief look at some of the distractions learners face and what the individual alone, or with the help of the training organization, can do to address them and maximize the learning experience.

EXTERNAL DISTRACTIONS

The big selling point to many e-learners is that they don't have to "go" to training, which often involves travel or reduced productivity. The big claim of e-learning proponents is that training can be brought to the workers' desktops. This may or may not be a good thing. Have you looked at your desktop?

If it's cluttered, noisy, or stacked with work demanding your attention, it may not be the best place to try to learn something new. The fact is that someone's usual place of business may be the least likely place for him or her to be successful, especially if the necessary training is highly detailed or demands intense concentration.

If you're reading this at your desk, look around you. You probably see a big glowing computer screen, papers lying there demanding your attention, a phone that could ring at any moment—any number of things calling you away from the task at hand. Each is demanding your attention, even when there are things you know you have to accomplish. Now assume one of the things you have to accomplish is training that you aren't excited about, are confused by, don't think is relevant, or doesn't affect your performance review, and you can see how distractions may take their toll.

External Environmental Distractions

External environmental distractions usually arise from the physical setting itself. Cubicles or other "open work spaces" may make sense for a lot of reasons, but they can make concentration difficult. Some of the main culprits are

- Incoming phone calls
- E-mail announcements

- Fellow workers dropping by unannounced
- Unfinished work within the learner's view
- General background noise

Systemic External Distractions

Systemic external distractions are subtler but frequently just as disruptive. Some of these distractions are

- Managers not setting time aside for employees to complete the training
- Company expectations and policies around setting phones or e-mail to "do not disturb"
- Meetings and other mandatory functions

INTERNAL DISTRACTIONS

Internal physical distractions frequently exist in the immediate work environment. They consist of things that the learner may feel are "more important" than the training he or she is participating in. This is all part of the mindset we discussed in Chapter 4.

Frequently, they are less often "things" than distracting thoughts, for example:

- Messages that suddenly have to be returned
- E-mail that needs to be responded to right away
- A neighbor's questions or conversation that seems very important
- Doodling to keep one's hands occupied

Internal Systemic Distractions

Internal systemic distractions have to do with worrying about the value the organization or the individual's manager places on the training and often the perception that because the training takes place at the desk or workplace, it doesn't have the same value as training events offsite or in "real" (instructor-led) training. Lapses in concentration occur because the individual worries or at least feels uncomfortable about the following:

- Workload and responsibilities not being met
- Ignoring requests for help or other team activities and feeling that people will not understand that training is going on at the desktop
- Being perceived as slacking off or Web surfing on company time

WHAT YOU CAN DO TO AVOID DISTRACTIONS

Take ownership of your work environment. Decide for yourself how important the learning is, and respond to the event like you would to any other important but time-consuming event in your workday. As we discussed previously, this involves not only doing obvious things like clearing your desk of obvious things like desk toys and pens, but documents you have been working on or other items relating to tasks that might demand attention.

Alert management and peers that you are taking part in a training event. Frequently managers and co-workers are unaware of what employees are doing at any given time, and this will help prevent interruptions.

Investigate other locations for taking the training. If your work environment is not sufficiently quiet or you sit in a high-traffic area, it might be advisable to find an unoccupied office or other location where you can access the training unmolested.

Prepare for the event before sitting down and logging on. Do you have water in case you get thirsty? Do you want to get your lunch out and ready to eat? Does your neighbor with the speakerphone know you're beginning the program? Take a moment to center yourself and get into the right mindset.

HOW YOUR COMPANY CAN HELP

Taking responsibility for your environment is wonderful, but we are not always in control of the situation. For those of us who take e-learning at work, there are things the company should do to help eliminate these distractions. Sometimes these are readily available; others may be negotiable if you really want to be successful. While it seems that many of the key distractions stem from learners themselves, some are based in the belief that e-learning, particularly done from a normal work location, is somehow less important than other forms of training.

You can make this training a priority by alerting others to what you're doing. Let your peers and manager know when you will be involved in e-learning activities and negotiate time to take them.

Your manager or training department (if you're lucky enough to have one) can help support e-learning efforts by doing many things such as:

Alert management when you register or are asked to take part in an e-learning event. Very often, particularly if individuals register or sign up for training online, it's done without the specific knowledge of their managers. Priorities, schedules, and workloads can be adjusted if the manager knows you'll be occupied for a period of time. Letting them know how long an event is scheduled to take, the importance to your function or professional development, and the time you will be unavailable can go a long way to reducing management interference with the learning process and give you more confidence that your efforts are being supported. Work that goes by the wayside or is deferred becomes less of a barrier to learning.

Find alternate locations onsite for participants to take computer-based training. Many organizations such as the U.S. Postal Service provide one or two individual carrels in a quiet room free of clutter in most of its locations. See if you can take part in e-learning without leaving your normal worksite, but avoid the distractions of actually being at your desk. This is especially helpful for participants who miss the classroom experience of physically being away from their distracting work.

Confirm company expectations frequently so everyone knows that e-learning does take place in your organization and that it is to be taken seriously. Some companies have gone so far as to provide signs that can be e-mailed to participants and printed by the individual to place on their cubicle that say "Training in Progress."

Set reasonable time goals and meet them. Negotiate the time involved in the e-learning program with your manager, teammates, or training department so there won't be any sense that you're "playing" on the computer when you should be "really working." If a program is modular in nature, take the program in short sections at a time, rather than try to get through the program in one sitting. It is far easier to concentrate (and get supervisory approval for) for a fifteen- to twenty-minute segment of time than it is for two hours when all they can think about is the work piling up. Whenever possible, choose e-learning that can be done incrementally.

Remember to control what you can control. You can't control other people, but you do have ways of reducing their ability to interfere with your learning.

Setting expectations (for yourself and others) and providing an environment (both environmental and systemic) that demonstrates a commitment to a successful experience are the most important things an organization can do to support the e-learner.

SUMMARY

If you take the lead and work with others to make the effort, distractions can be minimized or even (and not nearly often enough) eliminated entirely. The result will be a better learning experience and improved return for both your and your company's training investment.

About the Author

Wayne Turmel is a writer, trainer, and marketing consultant in suburban Chicago. He is the director of product and marketing for Communispond, a national performance improvement company. He has contributed to works by ASTD, the American Management Association (AMA), and various publications. His first book, *A Philistine's Journal: An Average Guy Tackles the Classics*, will be published in May 2003 by New Leaf Books.

Glossary

Asynchronous. Asynchronous refers to activities that do not occur at the same time.

Asynchronous Collaborative Learning. Asynchronous collaborative learning includes e-mail (for question and answer or comments), threaded discussions, and reviews of notes, assignments, and feedback.

Asynchronous Self-Paced Content. E-Learning content or experience that is designed for you to learn at your own pace, time, and space. The content may include a lesson, course, test, assignment, simulation, game, or reference document.

Bandwidth. While this term has a set of precise technical definitions, depending on whether you are working in a digital or analog environment, for everyday purposes it is used to refer to the amount of information that can be moved over a digital connection. It is typically measured in bits per second. Dial-up connections to the Internet are typically of lower bandwidth than higher-speed connections such as ISDN, DSL, or cable modems. It takes longer, sometimes much longer, to move the same amount of information over a dial-up connection than it does to move it over a high-speed connection.

Behavior. The actions that people take: what they do, how they act, react, and respond. Behaviors are overt, discreet actions that are observable, measurable, and verifiable by others.

Bias. A systematic tendency or persistency to evaluate something without regard for any actual differences that exist between factors being assessed. When bias is present, you base your evaluation on your own motives, assumptions, and expectations, which interferes with your objectivity.

Checklist Evaluation. A quantitative assessment in which the rater indicates the presence, amount, frequency, or order of behaviors, characteristics, or conditions during the performance.

Default. A given set of values that are to be used and no others are provided. The sets of assumptions we work under and the reactions we have in situations where we are given or perceive no additional information. Often, the default assumptions we use in a situation are inappropriate, given the specific circumstances.

E-Book. An electronic version of a book. Typically it is a small computer—the size of a paperback and a legal notepad—with a backlighted screen that allows a user to read, save, highlight, bookmark, and annotate text.

Group Grade. Occurs when the instructor issues a grade or overall evaluation based on how all members of a group worked collaboratively to perform a task or assignment.

Hypertext Markup Language (HTML). The authoring language used to create documents on the World Wide Web.

Instant Messaging. A type of communications service that enables you to create a private chat room with another individual. Typically, the instant messaging system alerts you whenever somebody on your private list is online. You can then initiate a chat session with that individual.

Job Aid. A piece of content of information organized for easy access or reference within a job or task context.

LAN (Local Area Network). A group of computers and associated devices that share a common communications line and typically share the resources of a single processor or server within a small geographic area (for example, an office building or home). Usually, the server has applications and storage that are shared in common by multiple computer users. A local area network may serve as few as two or three users or as many as thousands.

Learning System or *Environment.* The learning environment or the management system provides the functionality to find, launch, and view multiple pieces of content or courses. In addition, learning environments provide functionality that may be common to different content modules or courses, for example, registration, security, scheduling, reporting, and so on.

Monitor Resolution. The resolution of a monitor indicates how densely packed the pixels are. In general, the more pixels (often expressed in dots per inch), the sharper the image. Most modern monitors can display up to 1024 by 768 pixels, the SVGA standard.

Narrative Evaluation. A qualitative assessment in which the rater describes an e-learner's performance through supportive data or illustrative examples, either in response to predetermined open-ended questions or as a straightforward narrative report (often one or two screens in length).

Online Learning. A learning based on the use of computer-based resources. Generally online learning requires the use of the Internet for obtaining and distributing information. Online education programs often are based on virtual learning environment elements.

Peer Evaluation. Refers to the process of having peers systematically assess one another's learning outcomes (as specifically demonstrated in one or more learning activities) and comparing performance results to the objectives and measurement criteria established for the learning experience.

Performance Feedback. Information that is directed to a person concerning a behavior or set of behaviors exhibited by the person in the course of performing a task or activity. Feedback is one way of helping another person understand how effectively a task has been performed. Feedback also provides information and options needed in order to change a behavior.

Pixels. Short for "picture element," a pixel is a single point in a graphic image. Graphics monitors display pictures by dividing the display screen into thousands (or millions) of pixels, arranged in rows and columns. The pixels are so close together that they appear connected.

Portable Document Format (PDF). A file format developed by Adobe Systems. PDF captures formatting information from a variety of desktop publishing applications, making it possible to send formatted documents and have them appear on the recipient's monitor or printer as they were intended.

Rating Scale Evaluation. A quantitative assessment that consists of one or more descriptive statements pertaining to the e-learner's performance and judged by the rater by choosing a specific value from an accompanying scale.

Receptivity. A person's attitudinal willingness to seek and readiness to accept performance feedback. Signs of low receptivity are impatience, silence, arguing, defensiveness, inattention, nervousness, apathy, and overcompliance.

Simulation. A computer-based simulation is designed to mimic the behavior of a real-world entity or situation, an object (such as physical product), human interaction, process, procedure, physical environment, or ecosystem.

Spam. Unsolicited e-mail on the Internet. From the sender's point of view, it's a form of bulk mail, often sent to a list culled from subscribers to a Usenet discussion group or obtained by companies that specialize in creating e-mail distribution lists. To the receiver, it usually seems like junk e-mail. In general, it's not considered good netiquette to send spam. It's generally equivalent to unsolicited phone marketing calls, except that the user pays for part of message since everyone shares the cost of maintaining the Internet. Some spam is e-mail people agreed to receive when they registered with a site or checked a box agreeing to receive postings about particular products or interests. This is known as both opt-in mail and permission-based mail. (Spam is also a trademarked Hormel meat product.)

Synchronous. Synchronous refers to activities that do occur at the same time. Synchronous learning usually refers to events that involve an instructor and one or more learners engaged in live learning over the Web. In synchronous learning you are participating at the same time as other learners and the instructor, in what can be thought of as a virtual classroom. Typically, you can exchange text messages, speak to one another, view a common presentation, and share a common whiteboard.

Trait. A generalized term that is inferred from a specific fact or observed behavior. It is a conclusion that may or may not be based on a valid premise.

Virtual Learning Environment (VLE). Refers to a set of teaching and learning tools designed to enhance a student's learning experience by including computers and the Internet in the learning process. The principal components of a VLE package include curriculum mapping (breaking curriculum into sections that can be assigned and assessed), student tracking, online support for both teacher and student, electronic communications (chat, e-mail, treaded discussions, Web publishing), and Internet links to outside curriculum resources. In general, VLE users have either a teacher ID or a student ID. The teacher sees what a student sees, but the teacher has additional user rights to create or modify curriculum content and track student performance. There are a number of commercial VLE software packages available.

Virtual Reality. A simulation of a real or imagined environment that can be experienced visually in the three dimensions of width, height, and depth and that may additionally provide an interactive experience visually in full, real-time motion with sound and possibly with tactile and other forms of feedback. The simplest form of virtual reality is a 3-D image that can be explored interactively at a personal computer, usually by manipulating keys or the mouse so that the content of the image moves in some direction or zooms in or out. Most of these images require installing a plug-in for your browser. As the images become larger and interactive control more complex, the perception of "reality" increases. More sophisticated efforts involve such approaches as wrap-around display screens, actual rooms augmented with wearable computers, and joystick devices that let the user feel the display images. Virtual reality can be of two kinds: (1) the simulation of a real environment for training or education purposes, and (2) the development of an imagined environment for an educational or planning purpose.

WAN (Wide Area Network). A data communications network that covers a relatively broad geographic area and often uses transmission facilities provided by common carriers, such as telephone or cable companies.

Index

Pfeiffer Publications Guide

This guide is designed to familiarize you with the various types of Pfeiffer publications. The formats section describes the various types of products that we publish; the methodologies section describes the many different ways that content might be provided within a product. We also provide a list of the topic areas in which we publish.

FORMATS

In addition to its extensive book-publishing program, Pfeiffer offers content in an array of formats, from fieldbooks for the practitioner to complete, ready-to-use training packages that support group learning.

FIELDBOOK Designed to provide information and guidance to practitioners in the midst of action. Most fieldbooks are companions to another, sometimes earlier, work, from which its ideas are derived; the fieldbook makes practical what was theoretical in the original text. Fieldbooks can certainly be read from cover to cover. More likely, though, you'll find yourself bouncing around following a particular theme, or dipping in as the mood, and the situation, dictate.

HANDBOOK A contributed volume of work on a single topic, comprising an eclectic mix of ideas, case studies, and best practices sourced by practitioners and experts in the field.

An editor or team of editors usually is appointed to seek out contributors and to evaluate content for relevance to the topic. Think of a handbook not as a ready-to-eat meal, but as a cookbook of ingredients that enables you to create the most fitting experience for the occasion.

RESOURCE Materials designed to support group learning. They come in many forms: a complete, ready-to-use exercise (such as a game); a comprehensive resource on one topic (such as conflict management) containing a variety of methods and approaches; or a collection of like-minded activities (such as icebreakers) on multiple subjects and situations.

TRAINING PACKAGE An entire, ready-to-use learning program that focuses on a particular topic or skill. All packages comprise a guide for the facilitator/trainer and a workbook for the participants. Some packages are supported with additional media—such as video—or learning aids, instruments, or other devices to help participants understand concepts or practice and develop skills.

- *Facilitator/trainer's guide* Contains an introduction to the program, advice on how to organize and facilitate the learning event, and step-by-step instructor notes. The guide also contains copies of presentation materials—handouts, presentations, and overhead designs, for example—used in the program.
- *Participant's workbook* Contains exercises and reading materials that support the learning goal and serves as a valuable reference and support guide for participants in the weeks and months that follow the learning event. Typically, each participant will require his or her own workbook.

ELECTRONIC CD-ROMs and Web-based products transform static Pfeiffer content into dynamic, interactive experiences. Designed to take advantage of the searchability, automation, and ease-of-use that technology provides, our e-products bring convenience and immediate accessibility to your workspace.

METHODOLOGIES

CASE STUDY A presentation, in narrative form, of an actual event that has occurred inside an organization. Case studies are not prescriptive, nor are they used to prove a point; they are designed to develop critical analysis and decision-making skills. A case study has a specific time frame, specifies a sequence of events, is narrative in structure, and contains a plot structure—an issue (what should be/have been done?). Use case studies when the goal is to enable participants to apply previously learned theories to the circumstances in the case, decide what is pertinent, identify the real issues, decide what should have been done, and develop a plan of action.

ENERGIZER A short activity that develops readiness for the next session or learning event. Energizers are most commonly used after a break or lunch to stimulate or refocus the group. Many involve some form of physical activity, so they are a useful way to counter post-lunch lethargy. Other uses include transitioning from one topic to another, where "mental" distancing is important.

EXPERIENTIAL LEARNING ACTIVITY (ELA) A facilitator-led intervention that moves participants through the learning cycle from experience to application (also known as a Structured Experience). ELAs are carefully thought-out designs in which there is a definite learning purpose and intended outcome. Each step—everything that participants do during the activity—facilitates the accomplishment of the stated goal. Each ELA includes complete instructions for facilitating the intervention and a clear statement of goals, suggested group size and timing, materials required, an explanation of the process, and, where appropriate, possible variations to the activity. (For more detail on Experiential Learning Activities, see the Introduction to the *Reference Guide to Handbooks and Annuals*, 1999 edition, Pfeiffer, San Francisco.)

GAME A group activity that has the purpose of fostering team spirit and togetherness in addition to the achievement of a pre-stated goal. Usually contrived—undertaking a desert expedition, for example—this type of learning method offers an engaging means for participants to demonstrate and practice business and interpersonal skills. Games are effective for team building and personal development mainly because the goal is subordinate to the process—the means through which participants reach decisions, collaborate, communicate, and generate trust and understanding. Games often engage teams in "friendly" competition.

ICEBREAKER A (usually) short activity designed to help participants overcome initial anxiety in a training session and/or to acquaint the participants with one another. An icebreaker can be a fun activity or can be tied to specific topics or training goals. While a useful tool in itself, the icebreaker comes into its own in situations where tension or resistance exists within a group.

INSTRUMENT A device used to assess, appraise, evaluate, describe, classify, and summarize various aspects of human behavior. The term used to describe an instrument depends primarily on its format and purpose. These terms include survey, questionnaire, inventory, diagnostic, survey, and poll. Some uses of instruments include providing instrumental feedback to group members, studying here-and-now processes or functioning within a group, manipulating group composition, and evaluating outcomes of training and other interventions.

Instruments are popular in the training and HR field because, in general, more growth can occur if an individual is provided with a method for focusing specifically on his or her own behavior. Instruments also are used to obtain information that will serve as a basis for change and to assist in workforce planning efforts.

Paper-and-pencil tests still dominate the instrument landscape with a typical package comprising a facilitator's guide, which offers advice on administering the instrument and interpreting the collected data, and an initial set of instruments. Additional instruments are available separately. Pfeiffer, though, is investing heavily in e-instruments. Electronic instrumentation provides effortless distribution and, for larger groups particularly, offers advantages over paper-and-pencil tests in the time it takes to analyze data and provide feedback.

LECTURETTE A short talk that provides an explanation of a principle, model, or process that is pertinent to the participants' current learning needs. A lecturette is intended to establish a common language bond between the trainer and the participants by providing a mutual frame of reference. Use a lecturette as an introduction to a group activity or event, as an interjection during an event, or as a handout.

MODEL A graphic depiction of a system or process and the relationship among its elements. Models provide a frame of reference and something more tangible, and more easily remembered, than a verbal explanation. They also give participants something to "go on," enabling them to track their own progress as they experience the dynamics, processes, and relationships being depicted in the model.

ROLE PLAY A technique in which people assume a role in a situation/scenario: a customer service rep in an angry-customer exchange, for example. The way in which the role is approached is then discussed and feedback is offered. The role play is often repeated using a different approach and/or incorporating changes made based on feedback received. In other words, role playing is a spontaneous interaction involving realistic behavior under artificial (and safe) conditions.

SIMULATION A methodology for understanding the interrelationships among components of a system or process. Simulations differ from games in that they test or use a model that depicts or mirrors some aspect of reality in form, if not necessarily in content. Learning occurs by studying the effects of change on one or more factors of the model. Simulations are commonly used to test hypotheses about what happens in a system—often referred to as "what if?" analysis—or to examine best-case/worst-case scenarios.

THEORY A presentation of an idea from a conjectural perspective. Theories are useful because they encourage us to examine behavior and phenomena through a different lens.

TOPICS

The twin goals of providing effective and practical solutions for workforce training and organization development and meeting the educational needs of training and human resource professionals shape Pfeiffer's publishing program. Core topics include the following:

Leadership & Management
Communication & Presentation
Coaching & Mentoring
Training & Development
E-Learning
Teams & Collaboration
OD & Strategic Planning
Human Resources
Consulting